More Alive Than Ever

Signs In The Miracles Of John's Gospel

Forrest Chaffee

CSS Publishing Company, Inc., Lima, Ohio

MORE ALIVE THAN EVER

Copyright © 2005 by
CSS Publishing Company, Inc.
Lima, Ohio

All rights reserved. No part of this publication may be reproduced in any manner whatsoever without the prior permission of the publisher, except in the case of brief quotations embodied in critical articles and reviews. Inquiries should be addressed to: Permissions, CSS Publishing Company, Inc., P.O. Box 4503, Lima, Ohio 45802-4503.

Scripture quotations are from the *New Revised Standard Version of the Bible*, copyright 1989 by the Division of Christian Education of the National Council of the Churches of Christ in the USA. Used by permission.

Scripture references are from *The Harper Collins Study Bible, New Revised Standard Version,* 1989, 1993 (New York: Harper Collins).

Library of Congress Cataloging-in-Publication Data

Chaffee, Forrest, 1932-
 More alive than ever : signs in the miracles of John's gospel / Forrest Chaffee.
    p. c.
 Includes index.
 ISBN 0-7880-2350-0 (Perfect bound : alk. paper)
  1. Miracles—Biblical teaching. 2. Bible. N.T. John—Criticism, interpretation, etc. 3. Bible. N.Y. John— Textbooks. I. Title.

BS2615.6M5C48 2005
226.7'06—dc22

2005002906

For more information about CSS Publishing Company resources, visit our website at www.csspub.com or e-mail us at custserv@csspub.com or call (800) 241-4056.

Cover design by Wendy Muhlenkamp
ISBN 0-7880-2350-0   PRINTED IN U.S.A.

*This book is dedicated
to my wife, Judy,
who has been my soul mate,
closest companion,
and dearest friend
throughout all the years
of our marriage.*

Acknowledgments

This book has come out of adult Bible studies with the "quilt women" of a congregation in Boone, Iowa. These remarkable women were a source of many new insights. Their unique ability to share their spontaneous enthusiasm in the faith has encouraged and inspired me to write. I wish to say a thank you to Bishop Paul Werger and Dr. Jerry Schmalenberger for their encouragement and ongoing advice in the preparation of this writing. Thanks also to my wife, Judy, who helped in the editing and proofing of the manuscript.

In the process of writing this book I have discovered that you need the help of many people and many other sources and references. I want to also say a special thank you to CSS Publishing for all their encouragement along the journey. A very special thank you is included here to my editor, Becky Brandt. Her persistent insistence upon accuracy along with her ability to keep following through on a myriad of details made this book a reality. May all who read this book find the vibrant life power of our Living Lord.

Table Of Contents

Foreword	7
by Paul M. Werger	
Prologue	9
The First Sign — *John 2:1-12*	13
Joy Is Like The Rain	
The Second Sign — *John 4:46-54*	25
Trust Is An Umbrella	
The Third Sign — *John 5:1-9*	39
Hope Can Be Moving	
The Fourth Sign — *John 6:1-14*	51
Bread Is Always Needed	
The Fifth Sign — *John 6:16-21*	69
Peace Is Like A Flowing River	
The Sixth Sign — *John 9:1-41*	81
Seeing Is Getting The Mud Out Of Your Eyes	
The Seventh Sign — *John 11:1-44*	95
New Life Is Like A Grain Of Wheat	
Index Of Illustrations	111
Endorsements	113

Foreword

Many years ago, a seminary professor of preaching told our class to pay attention to our use of stories and illustrations. They were the windows through which our hearers would be able to see the meaning of our thoughts.

Pastor Forrest Chaffee has an amazing gift of using stories and illustrations to help his readers discover what he is attempting to say. Laypeople will find this text to be very interesting and easy to read and understand. He takes the signs of Jesus and brings them down to very practical and earthy applications of everyday life. One doesn't always receive this result from reading or hearing sermons.

Pastors will want to use this volume to do some gleaning for their own sermonizing. Often one can listen to a sermon and hear only one or two meaningful illustrations. Any pastor knows that members of congregations will remember those stories long after other themes have disappeared.

Forrest Chaffee has a wonderful and unique gift of seeing illustrations from his daily walk as a pastor. It can assist other clergy to look carefully at the conversations and incidents that are incumbent to our journey through life, and this should assist them in their sermon preparations.

I believe that you will agree with me that this book on the signs of Jesus is worthy of your time as a reader. Perhaps, you will find yourself "more alive than ever."

                        Paul M. Werger
                        Bishop Emeritus
                        Southeastern Iowa Synod
                        Evangelical Lutheran Church in America

Prologue

There are times in which we are not as fully awake and alert as we should be. Did you ever take an automotive trip and pass through a town or area and not know it? During the years I spent as a parish pastor in Iowa there were many journeys taken up to Minneapolis to see family or to carry out some business. The towns of Mason City and Clear Lake were about half way and often a stopping place for rest and nourishment along the way. As I drove along, I would be lifted up in spirit by the beauty of the rolling countryside and the changing of the seasons. At times, I would enter into deep moments of reflection and meditation. I almost hate to admit it, but there were times in which I would arrive at the Minnesota border and wonder what happened to Clear Lake and Mason City. Are there not times in which we are not fully awake and alert?

One of my concerns in life has been to live life to its fullest. One of my greatest fears is that I will waste or fritter away time and come to the end of life realizing that I had missed many a golden opportunity and in the process had often been not fully alive. There is no question about the fact that there are many things that keep us from being fully alive. Of course there are the problems, burdens, cares, anxieties, and worries that weigh us down. We can get discouraged and down on ourselves. The sheer busyness of our existence some days can affect our senses both internally and externally. As we move through the valleys and mountains of life we fail so often to experience the full gamut of emotions and feelings. We can eat too much, drink too much, and sleep too little. It has been estimated that only one person in a hundred is a fully functioning human being.

John Powell writes that by "common estimation most people realize only about ten percent of the world's beauty and hear only ten percent of the music and poetry of the universe. They are alive to only ten percent of the deep and rich feelings possible to human beings. They stumble along the path of an unreflective life in an unexamined world. They survive with only a shriveled capacity for giving and receiving love."[1]

For many years in my parish ministry I have been intrigued with the Gospel of John, which pictures Jesus as the source of life. Here is one who attracted people because of his magnetic life force. His was a life force that flowed outwardly through his spoken words and healing power. On the way to raise his friend Lazarus from the dead, he empathizes so much with the crowd and the immediate family that he weeps outwardly. He knew the gamut of human emotions. He experienced the agonies and ecstasies of our existence. Out of this gospel we hear Jesus say, "I came that they may have life and have it abundantly" (John 10:10).

This life force of Jesus, so radiant through his personality, was physical, mental, and spiritual. It is a force that was certainly apparent through the processes of his mind. Even though confronted with the questions of authorities that were devised to entrap him in his speech and to make him look foolish, the deep inward thinking of his mind and the words of his mouth left them speechless. The Apostle Paul reminds us that to be fully alive is to have "the same mind in us that was in Christ Jesus" (Philippians 2:5).

The Gospel of John is different from the other gospels. Its purpose is not to give a chronological account of the life of Jesus, but rather to weave the story and words of Jesus around seven miracles, which he calls *signs*. The purpose of the author is to present the life force of Jesus to us not only through his words but through what he does. These miracles or *signs* are meant to reawaken us to a particular force of life that can enable us to be more alive than ever. And since this gospel is written toward the end of the first century, the author is able to look back and reflect deeply upon the meaning not only behind the words of Jesus but the meaning behind his miraculous deeds. He is able to be very selective since he knows Jesus intimately. He is able to choose those signs that are channels of the greatest life force the world has ever known. As the author ends this gospel he clearly states that "there are also many other things that Jesus did. If every one of them were written down, I suppose that the world itself could not contain the books that could be written" (John 21:25).

It is said that most human beings can list on one hand the people who are the closest of friends, for it takes effort and time to cultivate acceptance and the comfort zone that enables people to really share honestly with each other. There is, of course, a remarkable aliveness that comes from being close to another human being, especially a person that loves you. Our author gives every indication of knowing the remarkable aliveness of this Jesus because he has known and experienced Jesus as one who loves unconditionally. He states emphatically his purpose, saying that "these things are written so that you may come to believe that Jesus is the Messiah, the son of God, and that through believing you may have life in his name" (John 20:31).

Saint Irenaeus in the second century stated that the "glory of God is a human being who is fully alive!" Our purpose here is to look at the seven miracles of Jesus in the Gospel of John and to see them as *signs* and channels of seven remarkable qualities of life that can enable you and me to be more alive than ever.

---

1. John Powell, *Fully Human, Fully Alive* (Niles, Illinois: Argos Communications, 1976), p. 30.

The First Sign — *John 2:1-12*

Joy Is Like The Rain

On the third day there was a wedding in Cana of Galilee, and the mother of Jesus was there. Jesus and his disciples had also been invited to the wedding. When the wine gave out, the mother of Jesus said to him, "They have no wine." And Jesus said to her, "Woman, what concern is that to you and me? My hour has not yet come." His mother said to the servants, "Do whatever he tells you." Now standing there were six stone water jars for the Jewish rites of purification, each holding twenty or thirty gallons. Jesus said to them, "Fill the jars with water." And they filled them up to the brim. He said to them, "Now draw some out, and take it to the chief steward." So they took it. When the steward tasted the water that had become wine, and did not know where it came from (though the servants who had drawn the water knew), the steward called the bridegroom and said to him, "Everyone serves the good wine first, and then the inferior wine after the guests have become drunk. But you have kept the good wine until now." Jesus did this, the first of his signs, in Cana of Galilee, and revealed his glory; and his disciples believed in him.

After this he went down to Capernaum with his mother, his brothers, and his disciples; and they remained there a few days.

> *A thing of beauty is a joy forever.*
> — Keats

There is an old hymn that states simply that "joy is like the rain." Like rain, joy is a soft mist that can envelop our being and soak our spirits. Like rain, joy can be like a thunderstorm that cools the hot, humid air of anger, anxiety, and stress. How well I remember the summer of 1954 before my first year in the seminary. In order to make some money for school I worked as a groundskeeper and custodian for the Lutheran Social Services office center in Minneapolis. It turned into a hot, dry, dusty summer. A severe drought occurred for several weeks. Although I didn't have to do much mowing, I pulled around hoses and sprinklers trying desperately to keep the grass and gardens green. Late one afternoon it happened. Dark clouds rolled in and the distant roll of thunder became a prelude to the flashing strikes of lightning and gigantic booms of thunder. The rains came in torrents licking up the dust and dirt in the gutters. It rained long and hard followed by a sudden cooling of the air and a spectacular rainbow. Joy indeed is like the rain. It can refresh our spirits and give us new growth.

In the Gospel of John we look upon the first sign and miracle of Jesus. It occurs at a wedding feast in the little village of Cana, about six miles northeast of Nazareth. Jesus grew up in this rolling hill country and how often he must have walked down through the hills some fifteen miles to the beautiful Sea of Galilee. Cana was the hometown of the disciple Nathanael. One day Philip sought him out and said, "We have found him about whom Moses in the law and also the prophets wrote, Jesus son of Joseph from Nazareth." Nathanael said to him, "Can anything good come out of Nazareth?" (John 1:45-46). These little villages were so familiar and commonplace to the inhabitants that a rivalry and disdain must have existed between them. Could anything of significance happen in these places that would affect the course of our lives today? We affirm that something *did* happen. We affirm that the joy that came into this wedding long ago can permeate our lives today.

For some reason, Jesus and his disciples were invited to this wedding and Mary, the mother of Jesus, had much to do with the activities. Some believe that this was the wedding of the disciple John, which would account for such a detailed description of the accompanying miracle. A wedding in those days was a great celebration that lasted for days. It was no little thirty-minute happening. The ceremony itself occurred in the evening, followed by a procession to the house of the groom that was like a joyous parade. For a period of a week the bride and groom were treated like a king and queen.[1] Since wedding festivities usually lasted a long time, things moved at a leisurely pace. Many guests arrived, including Jesus and his entourage. In the midst of the feasting and joy there occurred a problem that must have been an embarrassing and interrupting concern casting a shadow upon the joy of the occasion. The wedding feast ran out of wine, the very symbol of joy. Is it not true today that the problems, embarrassments, and the stresses of life can take away our joy?

For a few years, in the early '70s, I served an inner-city church in Minneapolis close to the downtown area. We were surrounded by slum areas and many of our members were poor. Although the black people of Minneapolis were only four percent of the population, they organized and revolted against their discrimination and poverty. Windows of many public buildings were either broken or covered with boards. Burning tires in the streets blocked traffic. We changed the locks of our church building every three months. Through all this turmoil, I have a great remembrance of the weddings at which I officiated. Although many families were poor, they knew how to celebrate and how to be joyful. It was a Saturday afternoon and I paced a bit in the little room off the chancel area, a place reserved for the pastors to robe and say their prayers before any kind of worship service. Only thirty minutes remained until yet another wedding service. Suddenly the groom came into the room. I could tell something was wrong because he was still dressed in his jeans. "Pastor," he said, "my tuxedo doesn't fit!"

"What do you mean it doesn't fit, didn't you try it on?"

"Well, pastor, don't worry. I rented it over here at a place on Lake Street. I'll be right back."

Only 25 minutes remained until the wedding was to begin. To make a long story short, the groom was back in record time. I even helped him dress and tied his shoelaces. Although the ceremony started twenty minutes late, the wedding party and attending guests were full of joy, especially the wedding party, because the groom was properly dressed.

At the wedding feast in Cana an embarrassing moment was turned into joy. When they ran out of wine, Mary who was very much involved in the arrangements, came to Jesus. At first glance Jesus seems to treat her rather harshly, saying, "Woman, what concern is that to you and me? My hour has not yet come." But the word for woman here in the original Greek is a term of endearment and was the very word Jesus used for his own mother when she stood at the foot of the cross. Mary knew her son and knew that he would do the right thing at the right time. When we travel through joyless valleys, we have in Jesus one who knows our needs even before we express them, and even when we don't know how to express our deepest needs, we can let go — knowing that Jesus will do the right thing at the right time.

Our attention now is focused upon a detail that is of great significance to the meaning of the miracle and sign that is to follow. Such details breathe with the conviction of an eyewitness account. Six stone jars were standing outside for the Jewish rites of purification. The water in these jars was used for washing dusty feet and dirty hands in a ceremonial fashion in order to be properly cleansed for the wedding feast. We are told that each jar could hold from twenty to thirty gallons of water. Jesus commands the servants to *fill* the jars and the author emphasizes that these jars were filled to the *brim*, as if to let the reader know that there was nothing else but water in the jars. When the water was *drawn out* and taken to the chief steward he gasps in surprise, "Everyone serves the good wine first, and then the inferior wine after the guests have become drunk. But you have kept the good wine until now."

At first glance, Jesus seems like a complete spendthrift and has made up to 180 gallons of wine. No wedding feast could have used it up! Why so wasteful? There is a sense in which God seems like a spendthrift. Even when he created the universe he created it so vast and immense that it can only be measured in terms of distances according to light years, the distance light travels in a year going 186,000 plus miles a second. But in this eyewitness account there is every indication that no wine was wasted. The water only became wine in the process of being *drawn out*.

What happened was that the embarrassment and stress of having no wine was replaced by a complete kind of joy that could not be used up. God shows us this joy through this Jesus who radiated such joyfulness of spirit that it attracted the crowds. Even little children wanted to be near him. God created us to be joyful. It is a deep-seated quality of life that is meant to permeate our being enabling us to be more alive than ever.

Something else here should capture our attention. Jesus used the water that was for the purpose of cleansing that which was unclean. It is as if Jesus says that he will replace this water of cleansing with something that is sparkling, fresh, and new. You can almost hear Jesus say at this point, as he would say to the woman at Jacob's well: "Those who drink of the water that I will give them will never be thirsty. The water that I will give will become in them a spring of water gushing up to eternal life" (John 4:14). The spotlight here is upon Jesus. It is as if he is teaching us as we look back upon him that through his life, death, and resurrection he is constantly replacing the old water and methods of cleansing. Through him we are so cleansed, forgiven, loved, and accepted that his great gifts of joy and peace, through his Spirit, permeate our being.

Even so we can be cast down in our spirits and emotions. Negative thoughts along with such things as tension, stress, worry, idleness, boredom, frustration, suppressed rage, insufficient sleep, overeating, poorly balanced diet, smoking, excessive drinking, inadequate exercise, stale air, or any other of the abuses encountered by the body, mind, and spirit can keep us from being fully alive. Joyfulness of spirit is a gift of God through Jesus that can be a contagious force in our lives. It can be *caught* like the common cold. The very word *catch* can be an acrostic suggesting some of the ways in which joy can permeate our lives.

1. One can *choose* to be joyful. Walt Kallestad is the Senior Pastor of the Community Church of Joy located in Glendale, a part of the Phoenix area. When Kallestad came here, he came to a congregation of less than 300 people and whenever he tried to

make any changes to enliven the worship and outreach of the congregation, he was met with great resistance. Nobody was going to change them. Several times I have heard him speak of how this spirit of the people produced anger, resentment, and frustration. After a long wrestling period in prayer he decided that no matter what he was going to love his people as unconditionally as possible and he was going to choose to be joyful. If he awakened depressed and discouraged he would say to himself as he drove to his office, "I choose to be joyful today." From my perspective, this joyfulness became a contagious force and today the Community Church of Joy is one of the fastest growing churches in America.

2. *Act* joyful. Clinical psychologists have stated that you can act your way into a new way of feeling, as well as feel your way into a new way of acting. Perhaps it sounds almost hypocritical to pretend to be joyful when you are not. In a delightful publication called *The Joyful Noiseletter* was the story of a medical doctor who stressed the importance of belly laughing. He said that every day he would stand in front of a mirror and do two or three belly laughs out loud even though he didn't feel like it. The result was that often this deliberate attempt to laugh out loud would produce genuine laughter and he would feel relaxed and peaceful inside.[2] One day I tried it and at first felt self-conscious and uncomfortable but soon the belly laughs were real and I felt good.

3. *Thank* your way into joy. As the old song goes, "count your many blessings, name them one by one." I have found it to be helpful to take a piece of paper and write down the things for which I was thankful, discovering that each item led to many more. It has been helpful also to seek out some people and thank them for something they have done. As a pastor in Cedar Falls, Iowa, I was having a dreadful day full of stress and busyness. After lunch I was rushing to a meeting of pastors in the area. Suddenly behind me were the flashing lights of a police car and I just knew that I had been speeding. When the officer came to the window of my car something came over me and I quickly said, "I am a pastor of that

church at 14th and Main and I need to make a hospital call." He smiled at me and said, "I'll be happy to help you get there quickly." With lights flashing and siren wailing he guided me through the traffic to the hospital. Needless to say, I was embarrassed and ran into the hospital and made calls on two of our members. Since these members were also close friends, I thanked them for their friendship and what they meant to me. Something strange happened. I no longer felt rushed and harried. I left the hospital joyful.

4. *Cultivate* a joyful spirit. Listen to joyful music. Think joyful thoughts. Norman Cousins, the longtime editor of the *Saturday Review* in the last century wrote about a serious illness that came upon him in 1964. In August of that year he flew home from a trip abroad with a slight fever. The fatigue and lifelessness that he felt was accompanied by a general feeling of achiness that rapidly deepened. Within a week it became difficult to move his neck, arms, hands, fingers, and legs. After being bombarded with tests there was no agreement on a precise diagnosis. There was, however, a consensus that he was suffering from a serious collagen illness — a disease of the connective tissue. In a sense, as he put it, he was becoming unstuck. "I had considerable difficulty in moving my body and in turning over in bed. Nodules appeared on my body, gravel-like substances under the skin, indicating the systematic nature of the disease. At the low point of my illness my jaws were almost locked." His was a crippling and supposedly irreversible disease with only one chance in 500 for any kind of improvement. Norman Cousins, in close connection with his personal physician, talked about the importance of positive, joyful thoughts in any kind of a healing process. They talked about the power of the human mind to regenerate and recreate even when the situation appeared hopeless. Recognizing the great willpower inside of Norman Cousins, his doctor allowed him to move out of the hospital to begin a program of exercising affirmative emotions as a factor in enhancing body chemistry. Norman Cousins writes in his bestselling little book, *Anatomy of An Illness*: "It was easy enough to hope and love and have faith, but what about laughter? Nothing is less funny than being flat on your back with all the bones in your

spine and joints hurting. A systematic program was indicated. A good place to begin, I thought, was with amusing movies. Allen Funt, producer of the spoofing television program, *Candid Camera*, sent films of some of his CC classics, along with a motion-picture projector. The nurse was instructed in its use. We were even able to get our hands on some old Marx Brothers films. We pulled down the blinds and turned on the machine. It worked. I made the joyous discovery that ten minutes of genuine belly laughter had an anesthetic effect and would give me at least two hours of pain-free sleep. When the pain-killing effect of the laughter wore off, we would switch on the motion-picture projector again, and, not infrequently, it would lead to another pain-free sleep interval. Sometimes the nurse would read to me out of a trove of humor books." In this process of cultivating joy and positive emotions, healing came to Norman Cousins and he was able to return to being editor of the *Saturday Review* for many years.[3]

Such a story reminds us that laughter relaxes the inward spirit. It opens the heart to the Spirit's great gift of joy. Yes, this joy is a channel of health, healing, and a new kind of wholeness that makes us more alive than ever. The book of Proverbs declares, "A cheerful heart is a good medicine, but a downcast spirit dries up the bones" (Proverbs 17:22).

5. *Hold* on to joyfulness. Make it a daily *habit*. Let the spirit of Jesus into your life. In the final analysis, if our joy is only self-induced it will not last. Only through the magnificent power of the living presence of Jesus in our hearts and minds can our joy be real and lasting. Think about it. The one who brought joy to a wedding feast in a tiny village turned an embarrassing predicament in a home into something refreshingly new. This Jesus, now alive forever, wants to do the same for you and me. His was, and is, a contagious life force of joy. On the night before Jesus died, he met with his disciples in that upper room in Jerusalem. With death and foreboding in the air, Jesus taught many things to his frightened and disturbed disciples. Finally he said to them and to us, "I have said these things to you so that my joy may be in you, and that your joy may be complete" (John 15:11).

Yes, joy is like the rain. It softens the hard ground of suffering struggles and licks up the dust of discouragement and anxiety. Joy is like a soft mist softening the heart and preparing us for new growth and new life.

Reflection And Discussion

Thought Questions

1. Why do you suppose Joseph is not mentioned as one of the guests?

2. Why were the stone jars filled "to the brim" in this account?

3. Why do you think Jesus performed his first miracle at a wedding feast?

4. In what ways is joy like the rain for you?

Agree Or Disagree

- Jesus was very wasteful in making so much wine.

- Miracles and signs are needed for our faith to grow.

Endnotes

1. William Barclay, *The Gospel of John*, Vol. 1 (Louisville/ London: Westminster John Knox Press, 1975, 2001), pp. 111-123.

2. *The Joyful Noiseletter*, award-winning newsletter of The Fellowship of Merry Christians, Portage, Michigan.

3. Norman Cousins, *Anatomy Of An Illness* (New York/ London: W. W. Norton & Company, 1979), pp. 22-54.

The Second Sign — John 4:46-54

Trust Is An Umbrella

Then he came again to Cana in Galilee where he had changed the water into wine. Now there was a royal official whose son lay ill in Capernaum. When he heard that Jesus had come from Judea to Galilee, he went and begged him to come down and heal his son, for he was at the point of death. Then Jesus said to him, "Unless you see signs and wonders you will not believe." The official said to him, "Sir, come down before my little boy dies." Jesus said to him, "Go; your son will live." The man believed the word that Jesus spoke to him and started on his way. As he was going down, his slaves met him and told him that his child was alive. So he asked them the hour when he began to recover, and they said to him, "Yesterday at one in the afternoon the fever left him." The father realized that this was the hour when Jesus had said to him, "Your son will live." So he himself believed, along with his whole household. Now this was the second sign that Jesus did after coming from Judea to Galilee.

If you can trust yourself when all men doubt you
But make allowance for their doubting too,
   — you'll be a Man, my son!
   — Kipling (paraphrased)

We now look at a second pathway leading to a more vibrant life than ever before. Such pathways are important because they put us in contact with qualities of life that, when practiced and exercised outwardly, produce inward results. As we walk this pathway there is developed within us the quality of trust.

There is an old story about a boy who grew up in the desert far away from civilization. Supplies would come by train and enable him and his family to live. As the boy grew he wanted to know about life in the city. One spring day, his parents decided that this would be a good time for their boy to know more about such a life. He was sent to the city to be with an uncle for a period of time. Since the family was poor, they supplied the boy with a packet of food and told him to walk into the city along the railroad track. They warned him to stay on the track until he came to the station where he would be picked up by his uncle. It was a beautiful day and the boy walked along the railroad track enjoying the beauty of the distant mountains and the spectacular flowering bushes.

A train chugged along toward him and because the boy was deep in thought he never heard the approaching train. The engineer began to blow the whistle over and over again. When he suddenly began to hear the whistle he jumped to the side only to have part of the train hit him, sending him rolling and knocking him out. The boy was rushed to the hospital and finally recovered enough to be picked up by his uncle.

Days later, the uncle decided to make some tea and placed the tea kettle on the stove. As the water came to a boil the kettle began to whistle. When the boy heard the whistling sound, something came over him. He rushed to the front closet, grabbed a baseball bat, went into the kitchen, and smashed the tea kettle to pieces. His uncle came running in and asked, "What on earth are you doing?"

The boy replied, "Oh, you have to stop these whistling things and destroy them when they are small!"[1]

This is a silly old story but I'm reminded that our minds and spirits can become like the desert — dry and lacking in abundant life. We can be weighed down with problems and cares. We can feel run over and run down. Our ability to trust and believe begins to deteriorate, and those doubts and losses of faith need to be dealt with when they are small or they will interfere with our ability to trust the Lord as well as those around us. Without the quality of trust the ability to really be alive crumbles.

We have seen how joy and laughter is a pathway that is like good medicine with great capacity for healing. Albert Schweitzer always believed that the best medicine for any illness he might have was the knowledge that he had a job to do, plus a good sense of humor. I couldn't help but smile when Norman Cousins wrote, "It has always seemed to me that hearty laughter is a good way to jog internally without having to go outdoors."[2] Now we embark on a pathway that is called *trust*. This quality of trust is important in a tough old world where life can be hard.

As a young boy in the eighth grade, I became a part of a youth choir in a church. This choir was directed by the pastor's wife who was full of joy and enthusiasm. Every Wednesday evening we met in the parsonage for rehearsal. Before we worked on the hymn or anthem to be sung in worship, we would sing fun songs and favorite hymns to warm up our voices. In such a setting we used to sing an old gospel song that still is sung in our churches and that I still find myself humming out loud. In the old song is a phrase that is repeated over and over: "Trust and obey, for there is no other way." These words certainly came to mind as I read the story and miracle of Jesus that is before us. The quality of trust is associated with faith and confidence as well as with reliance and dependence, especially reliance upon a particular person. In every parish that I have served as a pastor there have always been people that I loved to be with because they had the ability to inspire and reactivate within me trust and confidence. To possess this sense of trust and confidence produces an umbrella of security.

We look into the story that is before us. Jesus had been in Judea and Samaria and has returned to Cana where we are reminded that he had turned water into wine. We are introduced to a royal official from the court of Herod Antipas. This official is a man who is in desperate need for help because of his little son being very sick. In fact, death seems imminent because of a high fever. He lives in Capernaum down by the Sea of Galilee and although Cana is almost twenty miles away through the hill country, he decides to try and find this Jesus. Obviously, he has heard about the wondrous signs Jesus has been performing, particularly his healing miracles. If someone could turn water into wine and heal the sick it was worth a try. We cannot help but notice that there is a measure of trust in his heart. When he finds Jesus in the village of

Cana he begs him to come down to Capernaum and heal his son. Jesus seems to brush him off saying to him, "Unless you see signs and wonders you will not believe." How often Jesus seems to test an individual to see if there is a measure of faith and trust. Or is Jesus simply in the process of reactivating the ability to trust that is already there? Often we can have a measure of trust for those with a reputation and credentials. We can have a trust in a medical doctor or a great institution like the Mayo Clinic because of its reputation. Certainly Jesus wants this official to trust not in just his signs and miracles but also in him as a person. What is at stake here is not just the healing of the man's son but the development of genuine faith and trust in the heart of this official and his whole family. Though seemingly almost rejected, the official indicates his desperate need, pleading with Jesus, "Sir, come down before my little boy dies."

Jesus responds to the growing trust and belief in the heart of the official saying, "Go; your son will live." This official has a remarkable sense of trust at this point knowing that Jesus is not going back with him and that this healing, if it is going to take place, has to take place at a distance. He has to travel all the way back to Capernaum without Jesus, trusting in the fact that something good would happen. Since travel by foot through those hills was slow and tedious, he wouldn't get back until the next day. He had many hours to think and meditate about what could be. Certainly in his work in the court of Herod and in his home with servants he knew something about receiving orders and giving orders. Perhaps there was almost a sense of resignation about it all as he journeyed homeward. He had been ordered by Jesus to go. He had been told that his son would live. With fluttering heart, full of questions and doubts, he must have put one foot in front of the other.

When our son Jon was a little boy, I would pick him up and hold him high over my head. At first he gave every indication of being uneasy and afraid of falling. But the more I did it the more he relaxed and soon he laughed with glee when I held him high. One day, I sat him on top of the refrigerator and told him to jump and that I would catch him. Once again, he was very fearful but finally took a jump of faith and when I caught him he laughed and laughed. That was a mistake, for now he wanted to do it over and over again. In the historical account that is before us the official's quality of trust was growing and developing even as he walked home. He was taking Soren Kierkegaard's "leap of faith" without knowing it.

When the official arrived home he was met by his servants who told him that his son was alive and well! There must have been some question of doubt, some need for reassurance in his growing trust because he wanted to know when the boy had begun to recover. When he was told that the fever had subsided at one o'clock in the afternoon of the previous day he was astounded. Why that was the moment when he had been talking to Jesus. That was the moment he had heard Jesus say, "Go; your son will live." At this point not only does the official trust and believe, but his whole family as well.

There is a progression in the development of trust in this story that is a part of the development of trust in your life and mine. Robert Kysar writes: "trust is a process, never a simple possession."[3] First of all there is a trust in a person that is based on the words of others about this person. If we really want to know about another person, we depend initially upon that person's reputation. We depend upon what others have said and upon what others have written. We recently purchased a "double-wide" home in a beautiful court in Mesa, Arizona. The place needed to be painted inside and have new carpeting installed. Our little yard had, among other things, an orange tree, a pine tree, and a dwarf palm. Since the previous owners had moved away and had been gone for many months these trees were overgrown and tangled up in each other and desperately needed to be trimmed. Because we had purchased this home late in the season and were heading north to our main home in Iowa, we needed to know who could be trusted to paint, install carpeting, and care for the yard. We needed to find someone who would check our home daily in the heat of an Arizona summer. We discovered that we didn't have to look very far. Painters who lived in the court were recommended by others. A caretaker who lived in the court had the reputation of being able to fix anything and was said to be very responsible. Our trust in these people was real and based on the words of others. The official in the gospel story had a trust in Jesus initially that was based on his reputation as a teacher and healer.

Secondly, there is the trust that is based on the actual words of the person we want to trust. When we talked to the painters who were going to paint our house, we discovered in a short time that they knew all about painting and knew exactly what to do. They radiated an expertise that gave us confidence. They possessed a down-to-earth sense of humor and knowledge of how to approach a project and to complete it in an efficient manner. It was easy to call them "Dick" and "Louie" and, in a short time, they won over our trust. The official in our story went to Jesus first of all because he had heard about him and his reputation as a great teacher and healer. His trust developed when he personally heard the words of Jesus and then his command, "Go; your son will live."[4]

How do we come to trust Jesus today? From the time I was small, on my journey of faith, I developed a trust in Jesus by hearing the words of Jesus not only through the scriptures but through the words of Jesus through others. When I was about four years old, we had come to a tough time of life. My sister and I lived alone with my mother since she was divorced from our father who had completely deserted us. My mother developed tuberculosis and so her mother, my grandmother, often came to help. One day my grandmother fell and broke her hip and after a long period of hospitalization, since there were no present-day methods of pinning a hip, she came to our home so that my mother could help her. Things went from bad to worse. My mother was placed in an oxygen tent for long periods of time each day because of the advancing tuberculosis. My grandmother cared for us by walking around on crutches. Then, my sister and I came down with scarlet fever. The health officials came as they did in those days with a sign and nailed it on the front door. The sign read, QUARANTINED! CONTAGIOUS DISEASE. DO NOT ENTER. I wondered how we would get our food and who would help us since we were quarantined. One day, there was a knock on the door and our pastor entered our home. Pastor Moe was a person whom I had learned to love because when I went to Sunday school he would call me by name and when he preached in worship he told the most wonderful stories. Now he dared to enter our home. He came with a huge basket of food and he said a prayer with us to this Jesus I was just beginning to know. In a sense I heard the words of Jesus through this pastor in my life over and over again. In the development of the quality of trust the words of Jesus need to be heard through what we say and what we do.[5]

Finally, there is the trust in another person that comes through the actual presence of the person in our lives and in their words and deeds. We trust that person not just because we have heard many things about the person. We trust not just because we hear wonderful words from the person's own lips. In the final analysis, we trust because of what the person *does*. We trust because the actions of the person verify their words and promises. As we have mentioned, when we purchased our little home in Mesa the backyard had an orange tree, a pine tree, and one of those dwarf palms. They were all overgrown and tangled in each other. The trunk of the palm tree was covered with branches with very sharp protrusions that could easily tear your clothing and injure your hands. Since we had to return to Iowa, we hired a caretaker who said he would not only look after the house but would trim and prune our trees. When we returned in the fall of the year you should have seen our backyard. You could actually see the pine tree and orange tree. The dwarf palm looked like a palm! What seemed like an almost impossible job of pruning and trimming became a sight of beauty. Now we not only trusted the caretaker because of what he had said but we really trusted because of what he could do.

The official in the gospel believed the words of Jesus "Go; your son will live" enough to turn around and walk back home. However, only when he returned home and saw the servants running out to meet him, only when he heard them say that his son was alive, only when he heard that his son was healed on the day before, precisely at the time Jesus said, "Go; your son will live," then and only then was his faith and trust in Jesus an absolute conviction. When you and I can trust this Jesus with an absolute conviction we become alive more than ever.

Nowhere should trust be more important than in our homes and families and marriages. Indeed families and marriage would deteriorate and finally break apart without the quality of trust. Sometimes the world around us makes fun of marriage. There are those who ask "marriage is a great institution but who wants to be institutionalized?" In other words, marriage is looked upon as confining and like being in some kind of prison or institution. In our home there is a small plaque that rests on a library shelf. My wife, Judy, likes to call my attention to it at times. On the plaque are the words: "We've been through so much together, and most of it was your fault."

Once I attended an open house in our church for a couple celebrating their golden wedding anniversary. I singled out the husband and after congratulating him on their fifty years of marriage I asked him what the secret of their strong marriage was and the secret of his own health and vitality. With a twinkle in his eyes he replied, "Well, pastor, every time we got into an argument or I felt particularly angry over a situation I would go for a long walk. You know I have good health because I spent most of my married life in the out of doors." Then he added, "Seriously, pastor, we have had a strong marriage all these years because we took the time to be together alone. Our faithfulness to each other produced the gift of trust which was like a great umbrella of security no matter what the storm." Then he paused for a moment and went on, "You know we always worshiped together with our family. Our faith in the good Lord enlivened our trust."

Once again the word "trust" is like an acrostic that spells out what goes into this quality of life that enables us to be more alive than ever.

1. The first "T" stands for *truthfulness*. When you have a relationship based on truthfulness and honesty in all things there grows between people a sense of security and trust. Show me a marriage in which husband and wife are completely honest and truthful and one sees a marriage with a strong sense of trust that binds family together even in the storms of life. In our relationship to the God who has revealed himself through the power of the Spirit and the

always-present Jesus, we discover a person who says what he means and means what he says. We discover a God who has created the universe and all that is in it, including you and me. We discover a God who is the essence of truth and who has never reneged on a promise. After the great flood in the days of Noah, God stated that the rainbow would be a sign that God keeps his word, that you can trust him to never allow a flood to destroy all people again (Genesis 9:12-17). Jesus in his conversation with Pilate said, "Everyone who belongs to the truth listens to my voice" (John 18:37). It is the power of this ever-living God through the presence of Jesus that can strengthen us in our truthfulness.

2. The "R" stands for *respect*. Honesty and truth in a relationship lead to respect. If you can count on a person to fulfill what he or she says they will do, and if you can depend on someone to carry out what they promise, such people become respected. When the painters of our Mesa home said that they would finish painting our home in three days and then completed it in that time frame, we had a new respect for not only what they said but what they could do. The court official in our story was used to giving commands and having his servants respond to them. When Jesus said to him, "Go; your son will live," he immediately obeyed. He was willing to walk almost twenty miles with a growing expectation of what Jesus could say and do. When he and his whole family experienced the health of their son through the command of Jesus, they believed. They looked upon Jesus with awesome respect.

3. Trust is enhanced by people being together and doing things together. The "U" in the word trust stands for *unity*. In the early '70s I was called to serve a congregation in Cedar Falls, Iowa, with a strong Danish background, and, in a short time, came to enjoy their traditions like dancing around the Christmas tree and their annual ableskiver dinners. As the congregation continued to grow there was a need for expanded parking and education space. Since the congregation was surrounded by old homes, the only way to gain land was to purchase them one at a time when they became available. After much study, deliberation, discussion, and

even heated words the decision was made to merge with a smaller congregation and relocate. Once the vote was taken and passed the congregation rallied in spirit. It was like they decided in their hearts to work together, pray together, overcome divisions together, and build together. Their unity made it all possible and the result was a new dynamic trust in the Lord our God and in each other. This trust became an umbrella of security that enabled the power of God to do its work.

4. Now in this concept of trust the "S" becomes the *security* that enables great things to happen and the life force to literally explode. Without a sense of security, there can be no release from doubt, anxiety, and fears that keep us from being what God wants us to be. Without this security, there cannot be the confidence that enables us to accomplish what needs to be done. As the court official walked almost twenty miles back home there were many questions and doubts. Even as he neared his home the day after being with Jesus, even as the servants rushed out to tell him his son was alive, he wondered. So the official "asked them the hour when he began to recover, and they said to him, 'Yesterday at one in the afternoon the fever left him.' The father realized that this was the hour when Jesus had said to him, 'Go; your son will live.' " Then with this security in his heart he himself believed as well as his whole household. They moved away from their doubts and anxieties and fears. They became covered with the umbrella of security that comes from God himself.

5. The final "T" in this quality of trust stands for *thankfulness*. When a person is truthful in the words that are spoken and honest in the deeds that are done there is a growth of respect. Respect for oneself and respect from others. The ability to work together is reborn with a unity of purpose in our families and daily work. In this unity there emerges a sense of security that produces the confidence needed to grow and become what God wants us to be. The result is the rekindling of a new spirit of thankfulness. We become thankful for even the smallest things of life. We are thankful for the gift of a day no matter what the storms. We live in a world of

trust. We believe that no matter what happens nothing can separate us from the unconditional love of God.

Yes, when we travel a pathway in which Jesus becomes real and close to us, we experience this love for every phase of our lives. We walk a pathway in which the quality of trust becomes a part of our lives. We know with great certainty that no matter what the storm, and no matter how close the shadow of death we can trust in the fact that we are not alone.

Reflection And Discussion

Thought Questions

1. How do we know that the official in our story believed the word of Jesus?

2. In what way, if any, does the official show a lack of complete trust?

3. What was the result of the miracle in the life and family of the official?

4. In what ways does the quality of trust become like an umbrella in your life?

Agree Or Disagree

- It is difficult to trust many people today.

- Our trust in God would be stronger if we could just experience a miracle.

Endnotes

1. Opening story contributed; source unknown.
2. Norman Cousins, *Anatomy Of An Illness* (New York/London: W. W. Norton & Company, 1979), pp. 88-89.
3. Robert Kysar, *Augsburg Commentary on the New Testament — John* (Minneapolis: Augsburg, 1986), p. 75.
4. William Barclay, *The Gospel of John*, Vol. 1 (Louisville/London: Westminster John Knox Press, 1975, 2001), pp. 202-205.
5. Olavi Kaukola, *The Riches of Prayer* (Tucson: Polaris Press, 1985).

The Third Sign — *John 5:1-9*

Hope Can Be Moving

After this there was a festival of the Jews, and Jesus went up to Jerusalem.

Now in Jerusalem by the Sheep Gate there is a pool, called in Hebrew Beth-zatha, which has five porticoes. In these lay many invalids — blind, lame, and paralyzed. One man was there who had been ill for thirty-eight years. When Jesus saw him lying there and knew that he had been there a long time, he said to him, "Do you want to be made well?" The sick man answered him, "Sir, I have no one to put me into the pool when the water is stirred up; and while I am making my way, someone else steps down ahead of me." Jesus said to him, "Stand up, take your mat and walk." At once the man was made well, and he took up his mat and began to walk.

Hope springs eternal in the human breast....
— Pope

In the Gospel of John we look upon the third sign or miracle which shows us what can happen if we have hope and cultivate its growth in our minds and spirits. We are reminded again that this story is written, "so that you may come to believe that Jesus is the Messiah, the Son of God, and that through believing you may have life in his name" (John 20:3).

At a nursing home a group of seniors were sitting around talking about all their ailments.

"My arms have gotten so weak, I can hardly lift this cup of coffee," one said.

"Yes, I know," another said. "My cataracts are so bad I can't even see my coffee."

"I couldn't even mark an X at election time because my hands are so crippled," volunteered a third.

"I can't turn my head because of the arthritis in my neck," said a fourth, to which several nodded weakly in agreement.

"My blood pressure pills make me so dizzy!" exclaimed another.

"I forget where I am and where I'm going," said another.

"I guess that's the price we pay for getting old," winced an old man as he slowly shook his head.

The others nodded in agreement.

"Well, maybe we should count our blessings," one woman said. "At least we can all still drive!"

Although this is an old piece of humor there is a truth that emerges. In the face of so many pains and problems it would have been easy for these seniors to feel depressed, useless, and discouraged. Yet they possessed a remarkable quality of life that lifted their spirits and made them more alive. They could see good things in the midst of the bad. They could find things about which to be thankful. They possessed the great quality of life that we call *hope*.

We are told that Jesus returns to Jerusalem to celebrate one of the great festivals *of* his people. How he loved to be a part of the worship experiences and celebrations *with* his people. He wanted to be with them to share their joy and their faith. It was part of his aliveness that came from being with others. There is every indication again that this is an eyewitness account because of the details in the story before us. We are told of a great pool of water located near the Sheep Gate that was in the northeast area of the temple grounds. This pool of water was trapezoidal in form, 165 to 220 feet wide by 315 feet long, divided by a partition. There were colonnades on the four sides and on the partition. The word for "pool" in the original Greek was *kolumbethron*. This is a word which comes from a verb meaning *to dive* indicating that the pool was deep enough for a person to swim. Apparently this pool had underground springs and it was believed that whenever the waters were stirred up by their movement that the water had healing power for those who got into the bubbling waters.[1] How well I remember being in Jerusalem looking down upon the remains of this pool. It was located twenty to thirty feet below the present Jerusalem. In fact, the streets that Jesus walked are at least twenty feet below the present ones because of the destruction and debris of the centuries. Our attention is focused upon the invalids — the blind, the lame, and the paralyzed who lay around the pool waiting for the waters to bubble so they could get into the healing waters, or have someone to help them into the waters. One man in particular catches our special attention. He had been ill for 38 years. We don't know for sure if he was completely paralyzed physically, but he was certainly paralyzed in his mind and spirit. To him his condition must have seemed hopeless. In a sense he was a prisoner of his own despair. Yet, I wonder if there wasn't some untouched shred of hope that permeated his being. Maybe deep down inside there was a longing to just be able to get up and to take on the frustrations, worries, and pressures of everyday life. Is it not possible for us to succumb to our illnesses and destructive habits? We can give in to alcoholism, heart trouble, and partial paralysis. There is a sense in which we can retreat inwardly to avoid responsibilities. We can become more and more self-centered and literally long for and demand sympathy. In short, we become hopeless and lifeless. In any twelve-step program for addictions there is an emphasis upon recognizing that we are helpless and in need of some kind of higher power to help us.

In Dr. Phillip C. McGraw's book on *Relationship Rescue*, "Dr. Phil," as he is popularly known, emphasizes that it is important for a person to recognize where they are in life. Any change "begins from the inside out as you get back in touch with who you are and as you decide what to do with your love, your life, and your vision. Your clarity and your purpose must become crystal clear."[2]

Please notice in this story that this helpless and at least partially paralyzed man did not seek out Jesus. It was this Jesus who noticed him. He sought him out. He cut to the core of what was wrong. He knew how long he had been lying there and asks him, "Do you want to be made well?" First and foremost we need to recognize our helplessness and our need for help. All of us can come up with excuses as to why we are in what seems to be hopeless situations. When confronted with the probing question of Jesus the man in our story replies, "Sir, I have no one to put me into the pool when the water is stirred up; and while I am making my way, someone else steps down ahead of me." Talk about excuses! Could it be that this man was almost content to live in kind of a relaxed stupor away from the responsibilities and pressures of daily life? The only way out of this paralysis of the spirit was for him to be motivated to act, to take some kind of step that would rekindle his hope. Hope is a quality of life that enables us to look ahead and catch a vision of what we can be and do. At this point Jesus commands him to take action saying, "Stand up, take your mat and walk."

In my undergraduate days at Gustavus Adolphus College in Saint Peter, Minnesota, I took a course in Humanities from Dr. George Forell, who went on to organize and head up the School of Religion at the University of Iowa for many years. At the beginning of the course he assigned us a term paper reminding us not to leave it to the end of the semester. One day when we were halfway through the course he stopped and asked us how many had started our papers. Only one person raised her hand which gave me a momentary sense of relief since I for one had not begun. Dr. Forell cleared his throat and then said, "Listen carefully! I am going to give you four little words. If you will remember them and implant them on your brain and then do them you will be helped in all your endeavors from this moment on." He paused I'm sure to let this statement sink in and then he continued. "These four simple words are: *beginning is half done!*" He went on to tell us that we were not to go to bed that night until we had started our papers and emphasized that we were not to let good things keep us from doing that which was best. We were not to go back to our rooms and clear our desks or straighten things up. No, we were to go back to our rooms and begin our term papers. Needless to say, when I returned to my room I began the required term paper and discovered that just beginning caused me to get more done than I ever expected.

For this helpless, hopeless man in our story the first step was all important. Using all of his strengthened willpower he did something he never thought possible. He picked up his bed mat and stood up! It was then that healing health power poured through him and he walked. Hope filled his being. He could walk. He could do something on his own. He could look forward to what he could be and do. He became more alive than ever.

Yes, we want to use this word *hope* to describe a remarkable quality of aliveness. Once again let's use this word as an acrostic. Each letter can remind us of some of the ingredients that go into being a person full of hopefulness.

1. First of all the "H" stands for *health and healing* that comes through the willpower generated when we become aware of Jesus our Lord seeking us out. It can happen in a conversation with a friend. It can happen in our prayer lives. It can happen when we are listening to music. It can happen in a chance conversation with a stranger. It can happen when we listen to someone speaking. It can happen when we are reading and studying. Suddenly there is generated within us a kind of expectation of what can be done. Suddenly we look forward with a renewed confidence. When calling on the sick through the years, I have often heard doctors say, "There is nothing more that we can do. This person has lost the will to live."

At a workshop for pastors I heard a speaker talking about the will and desire for life. He spoke of an experiment with rats in which they took one rat and placed it in a huge tub of water. The rat swam around and around for a while and then just gave up and drowned. Another rat was placed in the tub and after a while was taken out of the water for a short time and then placed back. Somehow the brief experience of freedom from the water programmed into the instinct of the rat the possibility and hope of escape. The result was that the rat swam around for hours somehow knowing there was the possibility of new life away from the water.

The man in our story had been ill for 38 years. He was really paralyzed in his mind and spirit. He had no hope for anything until Jesus came, until he came into contact with a higher power beyond him.

2. The "O" in hope represents *opportunity*. The presence of this living Jesus in our lives can show us opportunities of new things and new exciting ways to serve. So often in our English language we use the word "hope" in a sort of wishful thinking manner. We say, "I hope the weather will be better tomorrow." Or "I hope my golf game will suddenly improve." Or "I hope I will meet the person of my dreams today." But the word "hope" in the pages of scripture is a powerful word, a word of absolute conviction. For example, in the Bible the hope of the life to come is not wishful thinking but an absolute certainty. In our story Jesus approaches the man beside the pool. We have here only a portion of the conversation. In his words Jesus must have stirred the mind of this man and given him a vision of the opportunities before him if he would only take up his bed mat and walk. He gave him a vision of a whole new way of life. He filled his life with hope, yes, with a conviction of what could be.

Through the years I have at times told the silly story of a woman who awakened in the morning and looked out the window, only to see a dead mule on her front yard. Horrified she called the rendering service to come and remove the animal. When the men arrived she came running out the front door and said, "Gentlemen, I have changed my mind. I will give each of you $20 if you will take this dead mule and put it in the bathtub in our upstairs bathroom." They were greatly surprised by her offer, but $20 was $20 they could certainly use. With a great deal of struggle and effort they finally got the dead mule up the stairs and into the bathtub. As they were leaving, one of the men couldn't help but ask, "Madam, I know it's none of our business, but why would you want this dead mule in your bathtub?"

She immediately answered, "Well, I'll tell you. Every evening my husband comes home from work. He changes clothes, puts on his slippers, sits in that big easy chair, grabs his pipe and lights it up, looks at the newspaper and then up at me and always asks, 'What's new?' Well, tonight I'm going to tell him!"

Friend, are you looking for something new? Jesus comes to us when we are tired and bored, depressed and discouraged, and seemingly unable to act. He comes to us when life seems hopeless. He comes with a new kind of strength that we call hope and pours it into your spirit and mine showing us new opportunities to give and to serve. "So if anyone is in Christ, there is a new creation: everything old has passed away; see, everything has become new!" (2 Corinthians 5:17).

3. The "P" in hope represents *possibilities*. We can get into such valleys that we don't see the possibilities that lie beyond the next hill. We can get so down on ourselves that we consider ourselves worthless and in the process we become incapable of action.

After my sophomore year at college, I had the opportunity to work with the city engineer in Saint Peter, Minnesota. There were several housing and street projects going on in the area requiring surveying and the setting of levels. One day the city engineer took me out to a beautiful, open, hilly area to set levels. It was my job to hold the measuring rod showing the levels for the engineer to make, which he wrote down on wooden stakes and pounded in the ground for the contractor and builders. My upbringing left me almost completely devoid of any knowledge involving the mechanical and building world. What the engineer was doing in setting levels in that housing development was a complete mystery. All afternoon the engineer set levels, writing them down on wooden stakes and placing them into the ground while I was holding the measuring rod for the engineer to look at through his instrument, sometimes almost a block away. Late in the afternoon the engineer turned to me and said, "Forrest, let's pull up stakes." For some reason I had never heard those words and I took him quite literally. As I followed him back up and down the hills to the engineer's pickup I pulled up those stakes on which the levels had been written. When we arrived back at the pickup and he turned and saw me with all the stakes in my arms he became livid with anger and cursed me out for being such a dunce.

That evening when I told my roommate what had happened he laughed so hard that he could barely breathe and then left to go over to the home of his girlfriend. Alone in my room, and pretty much alone in the dormitory where we stayed since it was summer and most students were gone, I became totally down on myself considering myself worthless and stupid. I just knew that I was about to be fired. I was convinced that I would have to quit school. After a dreadful sleepless night I forced myself to go down to the city engineer's office expecting the worst. But an amazing thing happened. The engineer called me into his office.

"You know ..." he began, "so you never heard of that phrase 'pulling up stakes.' The more I thought about it, the more I laughed about it, and the more I realized how careful we should be with how we give directions. In this business being precise is all important. You really are a conscientious, good worker and today I'm sending you out with that young man you really like to redo those levels. I really like you and I believe you are going to be great at whatever you do, so don't get down on yourself."

Wow! Suddenly I felt like a new person. I went out of his office walking on air.

Yes, there are the valleys of discouragement. There are even moments of great embarrassment. But through it all, new insights are revealed.

New doorways of possibilities open up and hope is renewed. Sometimes when you think you are a nobody and you get down on yourself there is, if you are sensitive to it, someone around who reminds you that you are somebody and that the God who created you doesn't make any kind of junk.

As you read this there is someone close to you who is really down on themselves and feeling hopeless. Your word of encouragement can put courage into their heart and inspire again the hope that opens up before them the doorways of possibilities.

4. In our word "hope," "E" reminds us of *energy* and *enthusiasm*. The paralyzed man beside the pool obviously was totally down on himself, and we can only surmise that after 38 years of being alone with no one to put him into the pool he was indeed paralyzed in his mind and spirit. There was no energy, no willpower left in him. Now it was Jesus who sought him out and reenergized the will within to get up and walk.

Even down to old age there is a need to be energized anew every morning. Norman Cousins writes about meeting Pablo

Casals, the famous Spanish-born cellist, in his home in Puerto Rico just a few weeks before his ninetieth birthday. Cousins was fascinated by his daily routine. "About 8 a.m., his lovely young wife Marta would help him to start the day. His various infirmities made it difficult for him to dress himself. Judging from his difficulty in walking and from the way he held his arms, I guessed he was suffering from rheumatoid arthritis. His emphysema was evident in his labored breathing. He came into the living room on Marta's arm. He was badly stooped. His head was pitched forward and he walked with a shuffle. His hands were swollen and his fingers were clenched.

"Even before going to the breakfast table, Don Pablo went to the piano — which I learned was a daily ritual. He arranged himself with some difficulty on the piano bench, and then with discernible effort raised his swollen and clenched fingers above the keyboard.

"I was not prepared for the miracle that was about to happen. The fingers slowly unlocked and reached toward the keys like the buds of a plant toward the sunlight. His back straightened. He seemed to breathe more freely. Now his fingers settled on the keys. He began with the opening bars of Bach's *Wohltemperierte Klavier*, and played with great sensitivity and control. I had forgotten that Don Pablo had achieved proficiency on several musical instruments before he took up the cello. He hummed as he played and then paused and said, 'Bach speaks to me here,' and he placed his hand over his heart.

"Then he plunged into a Brahms concerto and his fingers now agile and powerful, raced across the keyboard with dazzling speed. His entire body seemed fused with the music; it was no longer stiff and shrunken but supple and graceful and completely freed of its arthritic coils."[3]

Jesus our Lord placed within the man beside the pool a new kind of hope which gave him the energy to pick up his bed and walk. This healing power of Jesus affected his body, mind, and spirit. When Jesus comes into our lives he brings healing power not only for the symptoms but for the whole person. This Jesus who suffered and died and was buried experienced resurrection power. His new body exploded with energy, such energy that some associate it with the earthquake on that first Easter Sunday morning. Energy that rolled away the stone and enabled Jesus to walk into the world and into our hearts, placing there that great gift of hope that makes you and me more alive than ever.

The Apostle Paul in his letter to the Romans adds this benediction: "May the God of hope fill you with all joy and peace in believing, so that you may abound in hope by the power of the Holy Spirit" (Romans 15:13).

Reflection And Discussion

Thought Questions

1. How do we picture the setting of this story? What are the smells and noises?

2. What do we know about the man lying beside this pool?

3. What command does Jesus give him?

4. How long did it take for the man to be cured?

Agree Or Disagree

- All sickness is a result of sin.

- God cannot heal us unless we want to be well.

Endnotes

1. William Barclay, *The New Daily Study Bible, The Gospel of John*, Vol. 1 (Louisville/London: Westminster John Knox Press, 1975, 2001), pp. 206-214.

2. Dr. Philip C. McGraw, *Relationship Rescue* (New York: Hyperion, 2000), p. 2.

3. Norman Cousins, *Anatomy Of An Illness* (New York/ London: W. W. Norton & Company, 1979), pp. 79-81.

Other Resources

Roger L. Fredrikson, *The Communicator's Commentary, John* (Waco: Word Books, 1985), pp. 111-114.

Gerald Sloyan, *Interpretation — A Bible Commentary For Teaching and Preaching — John* (Atlanta: John Knox Press, 1988), pp. 78-81.

Robert Kysar, *Augsburg Commentary on the New Testament — John* (Minneapolis: Augsburg, 1986), pp. 75-78.

Raymond E. Brown, *The Gospel According To John* (Garden City: Doubleday & Company, Inc. 1966), pp. 205-211.

V. Eugene Johnson, *The Seven Signs In The Gospel of John* (Rock Island, Illinois: Augustana Book Concern, 1955), pp. 30-34.

The Fourth Sign — *John 6:1-14*

Bread Is Always Needed

After this Jesus went to the other side of the Sea of Galilee, also called the Sea of Tiberias. A large crowd kept following him, because they saw the signs that he was doing for the sick. Jesus went up the mountain and sat down there with his disciples. Now the Passover, the festival of the Jews, was near. When he looked up and saw a large crowd coming toward him, Jesus said to Philip, "Where are we to buy bread for these people to eat?" He said this to test him, for he himself knew what he was going to do. Philip answered him, "Six months' wages would not buy enough bread for each of them to get a little." One of his disciples, Andrew, Simon Peter's brother, said to him, "There is a boy here who has five barley loaves and two fish. But what are they among so many people?" Jesus said, "Make the people sit down." Now there was a great deal of grass in the place; so they sat down, about five thousand in all. Then Jesus took the loaves, and when he had given thanks, he distributed them to those who were seated; so also the fish, as much as they wanted. When they were satisfied, he told his disciples, "Gather up the fragments left over, so that nothing may be lost." So they gathered them up, and from the fragments of the five barley loaves, left by those who had eaten, they filled twelve baskets. When the people saw the sign that he had done, they began to say, "This is indeed the prophet who is to come into the world."

'Twas God the word that spake it,
He took the bread and brake it;
And what the word did make it;
That I believe, and take it.
— Queen Elizabeth I

We look into the fourth sign and see a miracle which so moved the crowds and the disciples that it is the only miracle of Jesus recorded in all four gospels. The very words of Jesus enabled a crowd of thousands of people to be fed and nourished. The very words and actions of Jesus are like bread that is always needed in our lives. Indeed, this bread is always needed today to enable us to be a people more alive than ever.

Words, words, words! How often we use them and great is their might. In the Bible the book of Proverbs tells us that "a word fitly spoken is like apples of gold in a setting of silver" (Proverbs 25:11).

William Archibald Spooner was a famous English clergyman and educator who served at the end of the nineteenth century and into the twentieth and was known for what he did with words. In his sermons and teachings he would reverse letters and syllables as he spoke. Words would come from his mouth all mixed up and he wouldn't even know it. For example one day he wanted to say, "The Lord is a loving shepherd." But the words came out as "The Lord is a shoving leopard." The congregation loved him and knew what he meant and just smiled. These mixed up expressions are caused by some kind of a mental deficiency and became known as spoonerisms. One day in teaching a class Spooner wanted to say, "I have a half-formed wish in my mind." Instead it came out, "I have a half-warmed fish in my mind." One Sunday, Spooner came into the worship center of his church close to the time of worship. The head usher approached him all nervous and said, "Pastor Spooner, there is a woman sitting in the front pew that has been reserved for some special guests. Would you please ask her to move to another place? We're a little uneasy about approaching her."

"Certainly," he replied, and walked to the front and bowed to the woman and graciously said, "Mardon me padom, but this pie is to be occupewed. May I sew you to another sheet?" She smiled because she knew what he really meant.

Now as we write of those things that can enable us to be more alive than ever we want to use words that can be understood and used in the best possible way. When we look through the pages of holy scripture we find that the words of our God have tremendous power. As we look through the selected miracles of Jesus in the Gospel of John, we discover that these words are full of truth and empowering strength. We cannot help but notice that the words of Jesus enable a person to act and become more alive. When the wedding feast ran out of wine, Mary goes to the servants and says concerning Jesus, "Do whatever he tells you." And when that official in the court of King Herod traveled from Capernaum to Cana to ask Jesus to come and heal his son who was close to death, Jesus says simply, "Go; your son will live." We discover that when the official believed the word of Jesus and returned home the next day his son's fever had broken at the very moment Jesus gave his word of command. In the third miracle, Jesus sought out the man who had been lying beside the Bethzatha pool in Jerusalem for 38 years waiting for someone to help him into the healing waters. When Jesus finally said to this man paralyzed in his inner spirit, "Stand up, take your mat and walk," the man stood up and walked and was healed. Great was the power of the words of Jesus.

Jesus and his disciples needed a time of vacation and rest away from the crowds and so they sailed to the other side of the Sea of Galilee to be alone. When the people saw Jesus and his disciples, they followed. Some walked around the northern end of the lake and others came across in their boats and others from the surrounding villages. When Jesus and his disciples landed on the other side they noticed people now coming to them from all directions. I don't know about you but if I had gone on a special retreat for vacation and rest and was interrupted by others, I think I would feel a sense of frustration and irritation. One cannot help but notice that according to the other gospel accounts Jesus looked upon them with "compassion" because they were like "sheep without a shepherd" (Matthew 14:14; Mark 6:34). Jesus knew the people were hungry and would need nourishment both physical and spiritual.

During the course of the day, Jesus taught them and healed them. As the shadows of evening lengthened he didn't want to send them away hungry. At this point, even a little Sunday school child could tell you what happened. Jesus took a little boy's lunch of five barley loaves and two little fish and blessed and multiplied it and prepared to make the distribution. The question arises as to how Jesus could control a crowd that is numbered as having 5,000 men in addition to the women and children.

Churches today are endeavoring to distribute nourishment to hungry people through international world relief organizations. There was a man known as "Gentle Ted" who was active in distributing food to the poor people in India through such an organization. Every day he would travel to the villages with his helpers. When their truck of foodstuffs would come into a village they would be mobbed by hungry, starving people and some would get more than their share and others would get nothing. "Gentle Ted" would feel each evening that he was a failure because he couldn't control the mobs. One evening before retiring he was reading in his Bible this miracle of Jesus feeding the great crowd. All of a sudden there leaped out to him from the story the words of Jesus to his disciples at the time of the distribution, "Make the people sit down." In fact the Gospel of Mark tells us that the people sat down "in groups of hundreds and fifties" (Mark 6:40). Well, the next day "Gentle Ted" drove into the villages and commanded the people to sit down before the distribution and everyone received some food.

Not a year goes by without this miracle being preached in our congregations and though the story is well known even by the children, it is always received with open hearts because we are all hungry for the nourishment that God can give. When it comes to preaching there is an interesting phenomenon that sometimes occurs. Like Pastor Spooner of old, we can mix up words and phrases and not know it. A certain pastor shared that once when preaching on this miracle he said, without realizing it, that Jesus fed the great crowd with *5,000 loaves and 2,000 fish*! At that point the head usher in the back of the church shouted, "Well, I could do that!" After the worship the pastor confronted the head usher and found out the mistake he had inadvertently made, so at the second service he really concentrated and carefully said that Jesus had fed the crowd with five loaves and two fish. Again this same head usher shouted from the back, "Well, I could do that!" Following the worship the pastor asked him why he shouted since he knew he hadn't made the same mistake. With a twinkle in his eye he quickly said to the pastor, "Well, I could do it with what was left over from the first worship."

This miracle reminds us that bread is always needed and that bread is a precious food throughout the world. It is estimated that in the Middle East three-fourths of the people live entirely on bread. Bread is said to be the principal food of the East and people are brought up to think of bread as having a mystical and sacred meaning. Bread is associated so much with the essence of life that for these people bread is to be broken not cut. To their way of thinking cutting bread was like cutting life.

In the days of Jesus there were two kinds of bread — wheat and barley. Wheat bread was the bread of the rich and barley bread was the bread of the poor.[1] Obviously, the little boy in our story came from a very poor family because he had a lunch of five barley loaves and two little fish. Many in the crowd were poor and longed for bread and nourishment not only physically but spiritually. The bread that Jesus had to offer was not only physical. In connection with this miracle Jesus in his teachings made one of his great "I am" statements saying: "I am the bread of life. Whoever comes to me will never be hungry, and whoever believes in me will never be thirsty" (John 6:38).

All of us have deep hungers and thirsts that need to be met if we are to be fully alive. We have discovered that the qualities of joy, trust, and hope nourish us and enable us to be alive. In our present story the crowd began to almost worship the one who could make bread and satisfy needs. We read that "when the people saw the sign that he had done, they began to say, 'This is indeed the prophet who is to come into the world' " (John 6:14). In the Old Testament we are told, "The Lord will guide you continually, and satisfy your needs in parched places, and make your bones strong; and you shall be like a watered garden, like a spring of water, whose waters never fail" (Isaiah 58:11).

There are of course those experiences of life that are like parched places in which we have deep hunger and thirsts. Problems, cares, stresses, worries of all kinds are a part of our daily lives. Sudden tragedies can so devastate us that we can wonder if there is any God who can nourish and sustain us.

It was early on Saturday morning when a fellow pastor came to the door. He had been serving as a part-time chaplain in a local hospital when the body of a young man, a high school student, was brought into the hospital. The young man had been at a party and had an argument with a young woman he had been going out with for some time. He became angry and left the party and drove off in his car at high speed. On a sharp curve he lost control and hurtled through a ditch into a cornfield. He was able to crawl out of the car and walked toward the road. In the ditch he collapsed and was rushed to the hospital emergency ward where he died of internal injuries. When the chaplain told me this, he added that I should visit the parents as soon as possible since they were asking for their pastor. It was 5:30 a.m. when I arrived at the home, and the first person who came to the door was the mother. The first words that came from her mouth were, "Pastor, where is God? Why has he deserted us?" About all I could do was to listen, and then listen some more. No question about it, she and the whole family were in a very parched place of life. It would be weeks and months before healing power would come and be the bread of comfort that would bring new life in the valley of terrible grief. In fact, it seems to me that there can be no greater sorrow than when parents look upon the death of their own children before their time.

Bread, physical and spiritual, is needed to sustain life. Physical bread of course is one of the most universal and stable of all foods. My wife loves bread but doesn't like the crust and will carefully pull it off and leave it on her plate. The *Journal of Agricultural and Food Industry* reminds us that all parts of bread are nourishing, even the crust! A crumb of crust is said to have eight times more of an antioxidant that may prevent cancer than a crumb from the rest of the slice (May 2003 issue of the *Readers Digest*).

God's nourishing, life-giving bread comes through many channels. Certainly it comes through *beauty*. It is said that beauty is in the eye of the beholder, so obviously there are different channels of beauty for different people. We are fortunate to live in a great country where all kinds of beauty can be experienced "from the mountains, to the prairies, to the oceans white with foam." We spend a portion of the winter in the great state of Arizona in the city of Mesa. We have discovered that most any kind of scenery in any of our states can be found in Arizona. This state and wherever you live has a beauty that nourishes the spirit, if only we could see and cherish it.

But beauty is not just in the eye of the beholder. It is also in the ears. Beauty is nourishing bread that can be heard through great music, and the beauty of music is in the ear of the hearer. Different kinds of music from rock to classical serve as nourishment for different people. In our family not everyone loves country music. But country music so often tells a story of losses and grief and is filled with all kinds of emotion. Someone said that if you played country music backward you would get your farm back, your house back, your truck back, and your girl back! Martin Luther wrote that "music can even chase away the devil." In the Old Testament we read about King Saul being tormented by an evil spirit. So he sent for David, the son of Jesse. This young David was known to be a man of great courage and one who was prudent in speech as well as one who could play the lyre skillfully. So Saul sent for David and hired him to be in his service. We read that whenever Saul had an evil spirit come upon him that "David took the lyre and played it with his hand, and Saul would be relieved and feel better, and the evil spirit would depart from him" (1 Samuel 16:23). Yes, the music of the lyre was nourishing bread.

And beauty can be found in the worst of situations. A young woman fell in love and married a man who joined the Marines and then was stationed out in California close to the Mojave Desert. She was able to come and live with him, but often he was out on maneuvers. They lived in a small shack of a home at the edge of the desert. In a short time she hated every aspect of her existence. The wind would blow and the dust and sand would sift through their place and was found in all the cupboards. There would be almost unbearable heat during the day, and she would shiver with the cold at night. She hated to be startled by the lizards and scorpions, and on top of everything else, she was extremely lonesome whenever her husband was gone. One day when she hated her very existence she wrote her dad and asked to come home. Back came a letter from her dad telling her that he understood how she felt but that her place was with her husband and under no circumstances was she to come home. Faced with such an ultimatum she sighed and began to look around and started to notice the beauty of the spectacular sunsets and the starry host at night glittering like sparkling jewels on black velvet. The Big Dipper and Orion became like old friends that comforted her and made her feel more at home. She drove to a nearby town and found a library and began to read about the Mojave Desert. On one of her explorative walks she found seashells! Now she began to realize that the desert was once covered by an ocean of water. She began to study more and made a collection of seashells. Her lonesomeness subsided and her heart burned with the desire to know more and more. To her, the desert became a place of beauty that fed her soul.

There is an old verse that says:

> Two men looked through prison bars,
> One saw the mud,
> The other saw the stars.

Another channel comes through our *relationships*. We are nourished by those who are around us in all circumstances of life. In the miracle that is before us Jesus treats his own disciples as family. He is willing to test and train them. He is willing to listen to their simplest suggestions. Like a father, leader, and teacher he tries to lead them into a deeper understanding. So in the evening of the day when he asks Philip where they can buy bread for the people to eat, Philip is stunned and says, "Six months' wages would not buy enough bread for each of them to get a little." Even Andrew tries to help but doesn't believe that anything can be done to feed the crowd saying, "There is a boy here who has five barley loaves and two fish. But what are they among so many people?" In the miracle that follows, he teaches his disciples that God can turn a little into very much. Jesus in the midst of relationships is strengthening and nourishing faith.

We, too, are nourished by family. We are taught and trained and tested. There is nourishing, strengthening power between those in close relationships. Dr. Larry Dossey, in his book, *Healing Words*, writes about love and healing saying, "If scientists suddenly discovered a drug that was as powerful as love in creating health, it would be heralded as a medical breakthrough and marketed over night — especially if it had as few side effects and was as inexpensive as love. Love is intimately related to health. This is not sentimental exaggeration. One survey of 10,000 men with heart disease found a fifty percent reduction in frequency of chest pain (angina) in men who perceived their wives as supportive and loving."[2]

A woman, still in her forties, had a husband who oftentimes was abusive verbally. After getting into it with a teenage son and his wife he went downstairs to be alone. Some time passed and the wife went to see if he was all right, only to discover that he had taken a rope and hanged himself. Months later this wife who had been a teacher for many years, as well as a close friend, came over to visit. The first thing that she did was to run up to Judy and me and say, "I need a hug!" In our relationship with families and friends I am convinced that there is healing power and nourishment in a genuine reciprocated hug. In the historical record of the scriptures we see Jesus healing people using the touch of his hand. Through the years as I have prayed with people in the hospital I have often placed my hand on their foreheads. Afterward, many of them (especially older people) would say, "Thank you, pastor, for touching me!"

In the 1970s, I was called to serve an inner-city church in Minneapolis. My predecessor, Daniel Martin, had been pastor of the congregation for forty-plus years, and when I came, they named him Pastor Emeritus. During my ministry we became the closest of friends and how supportive he was when there were tough decisions to be decided and new programs started. One day his wife became very ill and died within a few weeks. This pastor insisted that I preach at her funeral with the officiating bishop in agreement. Following the committal service at the cemetery, old Pastor Martin came up to me and hugged me with all his strength. He continued to live in the old parsonage and said he felt comfort in feeling her presence with him. Every day when he had a meal in the parsonage he would set a place for his wife at the table and would talk with her as he ate. What I discovered as I talked with

Pastor Martin was that the memory of a close relationship through the years was a channel of great comfort and strength to him.

Cultivate and cherish your relationships. They are a source of nourishing bread. And in these relationships there is the bread of *empathy*. We are nourished through our empathetic relationships with others. "Empathy," according to *The American Heritage Dictionary*, is the identification with, and understanding of, another's situation, feelings, and motives. It is the ability to feel along with someone else without over-identification. Yes, Jesus had empathy with the great crowd and their needs for enlightenment, healing, courage, and all their physical and spiritual hungers. He had empathy for their need for guidance and direction. Though the great crowd had interrupted Jesus and his disciples and their desire for vacation and rest, Jesus empathized and looked upon them with genuine compassion.

For the last five years I have had the privilege of conducting a Bible study with a group of senior women during the Wednesday noon lunch hour in a congregation in Boone, Iowa. During the morning hours these women made quilts that were sent to those in need through a world relief organization. They were amazingly efficient and could produce twenty to thirty quilts in a morning. As I write this, they have set a record of 34 quilts in a single morning. In our lunch hours together, they would bubble over with enthusiasm that would carry over into our Bible study together. In this study their joys and sorrows were shared. Arguments and discussions produced new insights I had not even thought about before. We grew together and became like family. In many ways it was an empathetic relationship in which we felt along with each other. I discovered as any teacher does that I learned more from them than they from me. Together we were nourished by empathy.

Dr. Larry Dossey states that empathy, compassion, and love seem to form a literal bond — a "resonance or glue" between living things, even in the animal world. Studies of animals and their relationships to humans indicate that empathetic connections of a strong bonding nature exist even if there is a considerable spatial separation. A parapsychology laboratory at Duke University has made a collection of 54 "returning animal" cases, some of them quite astonishing because there is no obvious way the animal could have known the way back home. For example, Bobbie, a young female collie, was traveling with her family from Ohio to Oregon, the site of their new home. "Although the family had made the trip previously, Bobbie had not. During a stop in Indiana, Bobbie wandered, became lost, and could not be found. Finally, giving up the search, the family proceeded without Bobbie. Almost three months later, Bobbie appeared at the doorstep of the new home in Oregon." The case study points out that this was not a "look-alike" dog. There was no question that the dog was Bobbie because she still had her name on her collar in addition to several identifying marks and scars. There is every indication that empathetic feelings between the dog and her family were a guiding and directing force almost impossible to fathom. If such empathy exists between animals and people, is it possible that empathy in our own families could even be stronger? Cannot empathy in our relationships be a marvelous source of nourishing power that makes us more alive than ever?[3]

Dr. Kenneth G. Haugk is a clinical psychologist who has developed an international helping-and-caring group known as "Stephen Ministers" who are now found in many branches of Christianity. In the training materials there is a great emphasis upon how to listen and how to care in our relationship to those in need, in order that we might be a source of nourishment to others. The training materials point out the difference between sympathy and empathy. Sympathy is important but is simply a feeling of concern for someone else without becoming involved in a close, caring relationship. Empathy, however, is feeling another's problems as if they were your own without actually making them your own. Dr. Haugk points out that if you were walking along and saw someone stuck in a mud hole, sympathy would be looking at the person and feeling sorry for their predicament. Empathy would be extending a helping hand to the person without getting into the mud hole with them. There is an old Native American saying that says, "Don't judge another until you have walked a mile in their moccasins." Empathy involves "getting inside another person's skin" or "walking in his or her shoes" without letting their problems become your problems. Empathy is remarkable nourishment, a special kind of bread that makes us more alive than ever.

Our *attitude* can be like bread that nourishes us every day. It is possible each day to choose to develop a joyful, positive attitude. As I write this, the State of Iowa is in the midst of the high school state track tournament. Dylan Davis is an athlete from Adel just west of West Des Moines who specializes in distance running. He has just won his third consecutive Class 3-A title in the 3,200-meters and is pursuing his third straight title in the 1,600. To him, running requires not only physical training but mental preparation. The attitude that you have as you approach a race and the attitude you have during a race is all-important. Having run the mile and two-mile races in high school and in college many years ago, I know that the attitude we have in training, and in preparing and participating in a race, affects how you run and how you act. Positive emotions and desires can enable us to do our personal best on any given day.

The story of Jesus feeding the great crowd raises a question. What is our attitude to bread, to nourishment, to the things we need, and what is our attitude to what we think we need? In the miracle before us we become aware of the fact that Jesus is concerned about all our needs, certainly our physical ones as well. Jesus teaches us to pray, "Give us this day our daily bread," and he assures us that when we pray for the necessities of life God will answer. In fact, the spirit of the petition is one of thanksgiving because God is always in the process of helping us with bread. Martin Luther, in his *Small Catechism*, writes, "Daily bread includes everything needed for this life, such as food and clothing, home and property, work and income, a devoted family, an orderly community, good government, favorable weather, peace and health, a good name, and true friends and neighbors." Wow! What a list of daily bread and nourishment.

Do you really believe that it is God's will for life that our basic needs will be met? Jesus, as he walked among us, could not help but notice how the crowds were worried about things. And, in an age in which famine and drought were always around the corner, they did worry about what to eat and what to wear. Jesus said to them, "Consider the lilies of the field, how they grow; they neither toil nor spin, yet I tell you, even Solomon in all his glory was not clothed like one of these. But if God so clothes the grass of the field, which is alive today and tomorrow is thrown into the oven, will he not much more clothe you — you of little faith?" (Matthew 6:28-30). The Bible teaches us that we are wonderfully made and that the God who created us, created us to be absolutely unique. God loves us and knows us intimately. He even knows the number of hairs on our head. My good friend through the years, Bishop Paul Werger, has had, as long as I have known him, a head that was mostly bald. If anyone would kid him about his baldness he would quickly reply, "God made a few beautiful heads in this world, the rest he covered with hair!"

The question remains. If God really cares for us why are so many people starving, millions of them in this world? I believe that God has placed us in a bountiful world so that our needs can be met and we can be instruments in helping others. There is enough for everyone's needs, but because of greed, lack of sharing, ignorance, and war, many are starving. Jesus is pictured in the Gospel of John as coming into the world not only to supply our needs, but to supply them abundantly. There is a sense that we can relax, knowing that God is in the process of providing for all our physical, emotional, and spiritual needs. After all, our God is a God of bread.

So often what we find stressing us out is not our needs but our out-of-control wants. We keep raising our expectations. Our parents were satisfied with a 1,200-square-foot home and a single garage. We want 2,000 to 3,000-square-feet plus double and triple garages. We have an increasing hunger and thirst for entertainment and escape. An increasing amount of time is spent on television and movies. The average American watches over 28 hours of television a week. One mother's fear was that her young son was watching too much television. Her fears were realized when she heard her son praying one night, "Bless mommy and daddy and give us this day our slow-baked, oven-fresh, butter-topped, vitamin-enriched bread."[4]

How well I remember when television first became available. We were satisfied with a black and white picture on one channel. Then came three networks from which we could choose. Then we experienced television with color! How I loved to watch the beauty of the Ponderosa on *Bonanza* in radiant, splendorous color. Now we have just moved and signed up for basic television that has over seventy channels and our main complaint is: *There's nothing to watch!* Perhaps our attitude should be more like Art Buchwald who once said, "I find television very educational — every time somebody turns it on, I go in another room and read a book."

Tony Campolo tells a wonderful story about a friend of his who had to take a bus trip across central India. He was in one of those old-model buses that should have been retired a decade ago; it was seemingly held together with string and glue. As is often the case with buses in Third World countries, this bus was crowded not only with people, but with packages, furniture, and just about every kind of domesticated animal.

Sitting across the aisle from Tony's friend was a very tired man whose neatly wrapped package sat on the luggage rack over his head. The old man wanted to yield to the sleepiness that was threatening to overtake him, but he couldn't, for fear that while he was asleep, someone might take his package. As he rode along, the old man would doze off from time to time. Each time that happened, he would wake with a sense of terror that his package might be stolen. He would quickly jerk his head sideways so he might check things out and make sure the package was there.

That went on for hours. Then as the man snapped out of one of his tense and momentary catnaps, he looked up to find that his precious package was gone. Momentary panic crossed the old man's face as he realized that he had been robbed. Then he smiled to himself, leaned back in his seat, totally relaxed, and fell into a prolonged and delicious sleep. Being relieved of the thing that had caused him constant nervousness, he had enough sense to enjoy being unencumbered. Tony Campolo adds that not many of us are that smart.[5]

However, something else is happening to America. There is a growing change in our attitude to bread. Millions of people are downsizing and enjoying it. What's exciting about this to me is that about one-fifth of the adult American population is happily living on less and enjoying it. Their numbers are increasing each day! This attitude to bread, this attitude to our needs and wants, this attitude to what really nourishes us is enabling us to experience new, abundant life.

The nourishing power of the bread of the Lord is not only for our physical needs but also the *spiritual*. Perhaps as you get older you notice that something happens to the ability to remember things. It is easier to relate to the old silly story about three older women who were talking about how bad their memories were. One said, "My memory is so bad that when I stand by the stairs, I don't know whether I've come down or am going up to get something." The second woman said, "You know I can relate to that. Often when I stand before an open refrigerator, I often don't know whether I'm there to put something back or to take something out." At that point the third woman said, "You ladies are really in bad shape. I think I'm going to knock on wood to give me better luck." So she rapped on the table with her knuckles, paused a moment, and then exclaimed, "Oh, excuse me, I hear someone knocking at the door." What we eat affects our bodies and our minds. Nourishment is needed not only for our bodies, not only for our minds, but also for our spirits, yes, even into old age.

One of the main points in the miracle of the feeding of the great crowd is that Jesus can fill up the emptiness in our lives that we are trying in vain to fill with things. Our spirits need the daily bread of meditation and prayer and the words and promises of holy scripture. When we pray, we need to pray not only for what we *want* but for what we *need*. We pray for money and things when we really need to pray for what we need in our innermost spirit, and what we really need is that inner security and that inner power that comes from the Spirit of God. We pray for success because it gives us status in the sight of others, but what we really want deep down inside is that inner nourishment from the Spirit of God that will give us a sense of fulfillment and satisfaction and contentment in all things. Yes, we need to recognize again those possessions that make us rich indeed.

A tax assessor came one day to a very devout man to determine the amount of taxes the man would have to pay. The following conversation took place:

"What property do you possess?" asked the assessor.

"I am a very wealthy man," replied the believer.

"List your possessions, please," the assessor instructed.

"First, I have everlasting life, John 3:16," said the man.

"Second, I have a dwelling place in heaven, John 14:2.

"Third, I have peace that passes understanding, Philippians 4:7.

"Fourth, I have joy unspeakable, 1 Peter 1:8.

"Fifth, I have divine love that never fails, 1 Corinthians 13:8.

"Sixth, I have a faithful, precious wife, Proverbs 31:10.

"Seventh, I have parents I can really honor, Exodus 20:12.

"Eighth, I have true, loyal friends, Proverbs 18:24.

"Ninth, I have songs in the night, Psalms 42:8.

"Tenth, I have a crown of life, James 1:12."

The tax assessor closed his book, and said, "Truly you are a very rich man, but your property is not subject to taxation" (author unknown).

Jesus amazed the thousands of people in the crowd when he provided for their physical needs by turning a little lunch into so much bread that there were twelve baskets left over. Yet his presence and teachings also fed their spirits. And it is true today! Jesus knows that our human needs go much deeper than the physical. All of us have spiritual needs that leave us constantly yearning for something more. We try to satisfy this yearning with physical food, with money, with work, with status symbols, and with sensuality. Still we are empty. In this fourth sign and miracle Jesus is claiming that he can fill the emptiness, that he can satisfy our deepest hungers, and that we can be more alive than ever. And he does this not only with the power of his presence, but also through the power of his words.

Reflection And Discussion

Thought Questions

1. What was the main concern of Jesus when he saw the great crowd?

2. Why does Jesus ask Philip about getting enough bread and what was his response?

3. What was the solution that Andrew offered to the problem? Why?

4. How would you describe the faith of Andrew and Philip in this story?

5. If you were Andrew or Philip what would you have done to help Jesus?

Agree Or Disagree

- We are what we eat.

- How we serve a meal and how we receive a meal reflects who we are.

- If God were really a God of love there wouldn't be so many hungry people.

Endnotes

1. Fred H. Wight, *Manners and Customs of Bible Lands* (Chicago: Moody Press, 1953), pp. 44-48.

2. Larry Dossey, M.D., *Healing Words* (San Francisco: Harper San Francisco, 1993), pp. 109-117.

3. *Ibid.*

4. Paul Slansky, *The Clothes Have No Emperor* (New York: Fireside Books/ Simon & Schuster, 1989).

5. Tony Campolo, *Carpe Diem* (Dallas: Word Publishing, 1998), p. 122.

Other Resources

William Barclay, *The New Daily Bible Study Bible, The Gospel of John*, Vol. 1 (Louisville/London: Westminster John Knox Press, 1975, 2001), pp. 233-241.

Robert Kysar, *Augsburg Commentary on the New Testament — John* (Minneapolis: Augsburg Publishing House, 1986), pp. 89-93.

Roger L. Fredrikson, *The Communicator's Commentary, John* (Waco: Word Books, 1985), pp. 124-126.

Raymond E. Brown, *The Gospel According to John I-XII* (Garden City, New York: Doubleday & Company, Inc., 1966), pp. 235-250.

The Fifth Sign — *John 6:16-21*

Peace Is Like A Flowing River

> *When evening came, his disciples went down to the sea, got into a boat, and started across the sea to Capernaum. It was now dark, and Jesus had not yet come to them. The sea became rough because a strong wind was blowing. When they had rowed about three or four miles, they saw Jesus walking on the sea and coming near the boat, and they were terrified. But he said to them, "It is I; do not be afraid." Then they wanted to take him into the boat, and immediately the boat reached the land toward which they were going.*

> *In his will is our peace.*
> — Dante

As a boy living in Fargo, North Dakota, I would spend summers out on the prairie land in the central part of the state, and I knew about storms. There was a terrible drought through those years and a great depression gripped the land and people. Those were the years of destructive dust storms. Great clouds of prairie soil would gather in the skies covering the sun. An eerie greenish color would fill the air and it would turn dark at noon. The dust would fall everywhere and drift against the curbs and in the ditches out in the open country. The mounds of dust were like gray and blackened snow. High winds would make it difficult to walk outside with your eyes open.

It seemed that the wind was always blowing out on the prairies during the hot summers. In the little town where I lived with my great grandmother, the standard joke was, "Yes, one day the wind did stop blowing during the noon hour and everyone fell down!" Thunderheads would form in the late afternoon and rise miles high in the sky. Their tips would twist and turn, rising and falling in awesome fashion. At times they would darken as the lightning flashed and thunder rolled. As darkness gathered, heat lightning would roll along the fields. High winds and driving rain and sometimes golf ball size hail would do great damage. In our yard was a grove of cottonwoods that would sigh and groan in the midst of great storms. Huge branches would break and rush down the gravel roads past our home, and in a few minutes they would come back from the opposite direction. These mighty storms were always followed by a great calm. Spectacular rainbows would fill the sky and once again a song of peace would fill the land.

The fifth miracle and sign takes place in the midst of a storm on the Sea of Galilee. This body of water is shaped like a harp and is thirteen miles long, seven miles wide, 130-157 feet deep, and 32 miles in circumference. The lake itself is located 686 feet below sea level, producing a semi-tropical climate soothed by cool breezes off the lake. The water is sparkling clear and pure, and generally calm.

During the days of Jesus, Galilee was the center of roads going in all directions. The great fertility of the valley and its beauty along with the hot springs of Tiberias drew a considerable population. It is hard to believe when you travel there today that there were nine bustling cities located around the lake.

George Adam Smith, in 1894, described the lake in this fashion: "Sweet water full of fish, a surface of sparkling blue. The Lake of Galilee is at once food, drink, and air, a rest to the eye, coolness in the heat, an escape from the crowd. Where there are now no trees, there were great woods, where there are marshes, there were noble gardens, where there is but one boat, there were fleets of sail."[1]

When my daughter Kris and I visited Israel and Jordan in 1988, we spent some time in the city of Tiberias on the western shore of this beautiful Lake of Galilee. You could walk along the paved road situated just off the lake and see many a fishing boat loaded with fish and nets. Restaurants served generous portions of "Peter fish," and the entertainment spots featured many a musical group and singing and dancing people of all ages. Soldiers casually walked through the streets finding relaxation and recreation from the horrors of violence in the Jerusalem area. One morning, an excursion boat took us to the other side of the lake to the site of what was the great city of Capernaum in the days of Jesus. As I looked at the high rugged hills in the distance I thought of the great winds and storms that can still pummel this place of calmness and peace. We were told that to this day the winds are siphoned down through the valleys and gullies around the lake and produce fierce storms with shrieking winds and high waves.

During the days of Jesus it was in the midst of one of these storms that we find the setting for the fifth sign in which there was experienced the great gift of peace. It is this peace that is meant to flow like a river through our inward being even in the midst of the storms of life. Such a gift of peace enables us to be more alive than ever.

There is an old story about an artist who was commissioned to paint a picture that would represent peace. When the painting was completed, those who looked at it were surprised because it was not a picture of pasture land with grazing cattle or sheep with sunshine filtering through wooded hillsides ablaze with color. Nor was it a picture of a shimmering lake surrounded with beautiful pines and mountain peaks spotted with snow. Rather it was a picture of a storm. In the midst of thunder, lightning, and pelting rain there was a waterfall cascading over some rugged cliffs. Growing out from one of the crevices in the cliffs was a tree with its limbs stretching out over the waterfall and ragged rocks below. Precariously placed in one of the branches was a nest with a small bird with its head uplifted and singing a song. The artist's concept of peace was a song being sung in the midst of roaring danger.

Look into our story containing the fifth sign. Following the feeding of the great crowd with a little boy's lunch of five barley loaves and two fish, the people considered Jesus some kind of a great prophet. The people rushed toward him clamoring to make him their king. The account states that they were "about to come and take him by force ..." (John 6:15). Jesus withdrew from them and walked up into the high hills overlooking the lake to meditate and pray. As the darkness descended, there was a full moon since it was the time of the great Passover festival. In the moonlight he could look down upon the lake and see his disciples in a boat struggling against the high waves, because a strong wind was blowing and a storm brewing. Here the author, as an old fisherman, can feel the sights and sounds of the past. Through the eyes of his mind and his writing, you and I can feel the darkness of the night and see the gray silver of the moonlight. We, too, can feel the rough oars with our hands, and hear the flapping sails, the shrieking wind, and the surging water.[2]

When the disciples had rowed about three or four miles, they noticed through the wind and waves and misty air a ghostly figure coming toward them walking on the water. To their superstitious minds the figure seemed to be some kind of apparition or spirit and they were terrified. Then they heard the cry of Jesus saying to them, "It is I, do not be afraid." But not all of the disciples were completely reassured. Big, bold, brash Peter cried out, "If it is you command me to come to you on the water." Jesus told him to come, so Peter got out of the boat and started walking on the water toward Jesus. Soon his heart was gripped with fear and doubt because of the wind and waves and he began to sink into the stormy sea (Matthew 14:22-33).[3]

As a young boy, we went to a church that had a painting above the altar of Peter floundering in the stormy sea, reaching out, and grabbing Jesus. But the historical account tells us that it was the other way around. Jesus reached out and grabbed Peter and saved him. It was Jesus who gave reassurance and peace to Peter and the other disciples. They were so reassured by the voice and presence of Jesus that though the storm continued they were able to land the boat. In the midst of the storm they experienced the great gift of peace that enabled them to act. This peace, indeed, was like a river flowing through them. Such a historical account reminds us of the words of the psalmist: "Then they were glad because they had quiet and the Lord brought them to their desired haven" (Psalm 107:30).

This Jesus, as he walked on earth, possessed a remarkable quality of life that has endowed him with universal appeal. The world has not forgotten him. His name is on someone's lips every second of time. In fact, time is dated from his birth. A billion plus human beings today claim to be his followers, and most of them are convinced that he is the one who can give them abundant life now and in the world to come. Through him in the midst of the storms of our life comes a particular quality that can enable us to be more alive than ever. Yes, we call this gift *peace*; that is a deep inner sense of calmness, poise, reassurance, and courage that enables us to act and to come alive as never before.[4]

On the night before Jesus died he met with his disciples in that upper room in Jerusalem. The disciples were filled with fear. The very night air around them was filled with death and danger. Together at that supper of the Passover meal Jesus taught them many things and then he said to them, *"Peace I leave with you, my peace I give to you. I do not give to you as the world gives. Do not let your hearts be troubled, and do not let them be afraid"* (John 14:27).

Today there remains all around us the enemies of peace. There are forces that disrupt the flow of peace through our lives. In this busy, pressurized age there are worries, anxieties, and fears that keep us from inward peace even into old age. There are those days of troubles and heartaches that make a sense of peace very difficult.

A commercial airline pilot on one occasion made a particularly bad landing. The wheels of the big jet hit the runway with a jarring thud. Afterward, the airline had a policy that required that the pilot stand at the door while the passengers exited. He was to give each of them a smile and say, "Thanks for flying with us today." In light of his bad landing, he had a hard time looking the passengers in the eye, thinking that someone would have a smart comment, but no one seemed annoyed.

Finally everyone had gotten off except for one little old lady walking with a cane. She approached the pilot and asked, "Sonny, mind if I ask you a question?"

"Why no ma'am, what is it?" said the pilot bravely.

"Did we land," she asked, "or were we shot down?"

There are days in which we feel shot down. There are days in which worries, anxieties, and fears produce stress in our lives that weakens the abundant life force we were meant to have. Stress, for example, is your husband losing his job when you have two children to support. That's what Amy Mahoney-Casp, 35, of Mesa, Arizona, had been dealing with for several months. She discovered that she and her husband Jamie had different ways of coping. Amy states that when "Jamie lost his job I retreated to what I call my cave. I resorted to handling the true basics with minimal effort elsewhere — no phone and no e-mail. This helped clear my plate and conserve energy in an attempt to strategize the situation."

Jamie handles stress differently. Rather than retreat, he tackles a problem straight on. "Experience has taught me that if you give it your best shot, it'll turn out all right in the end. The longer you let something sit there, the bigger it grows. It won't go away, so you might as well deal with it head on."[5]

Author Georgia Witkin states that the lives of men and women may be equally stressful, but many of the stresses, symptoms, and coping mechanisms are different. The fact remains that worries and fears produced by stressful events destroy a sense of inner peace and are harmful and damaging to our physical well-being. Stress can cause high blood pressure, high cholesterol levels, heart attacks, ulcers, alcoholism, depression, melancholy, and sexual dysfunction.[6] It is interesting to me that the ten most stressful events in a "Social Readjustment Rating Scale" are as follows:

- Death of a spouse or child,
- Divorce,
- Losing a job,
- Pregnancy problems,
- Revision of present habits,
- Son or daughter leaving home,
- Sexual difficulties,
- Marriage,
- Retirement, and
- Christmas and major holidays.[7]

Many experts in the field of counseling offer us what can be termed a first aid for short-term stress that consists of the following methods.

1. *Exercise:* Make sure it is regular and convenient. Walking is the most common aerobic exercise for men and women of all ages.
2. *Soothing environments:* Take a warm bath, a hot shower, or a five-minute nap in the sunshine. Things like browsing in a bookstore can create a soothing environment.
3. *Reorganize:* Clean out your closet, rearrange your tool chest, or set up a new tax record sheet. Any act of organization will increase your sense of control. As a sense of control increases, stress decreases.
4. *Play:* Don't just send your children out to play — join them. Play games such as backgammon for distraction, cards for socialization, and word games for self-improvement.
5. *Meditation and deep relaxation:* Detaching yourself from worries and preoccupations for at least ten minutes to thirty minutes can do wonders. All you need is a chair and a darkened room. Focus on an object or spot on a wall and count backward from 100, concentrating on your breathing.[8]

When it comes to stress and a lack of inner peace, we need something more than just first aid. Certainly it is important to add to our meditation moments the power of prayer. I know of a man who, when he is all stressed out, approaches God with his hands stretched out and facing upward. "Here," he says, "are all my problems and worries and anxieties and fears." Then he turns his hands downward as if he were casting all his cares away. Then he turns his hands upward and says, "Now pour into me your great gift of peace."

In the teachings of Jesus there is offered to us a great antidote for worry and anxiety and fear. The crowds of people who surrounded him were full of anxieties and fears. They were plagued with worry and stress. Certainly they were worried about food and clothing and for good reason. They were a people of the land who were only a storm or a drought away from complete poverty and starvation. Jesus tells them to look around and consider the birds of the air and the flowers of the field who didn't plant or harvest. Even so, Jesus said that if one little bird falls to the ground, God our Father knows it, and the flowers of the field were arrayed more beautifully than King Solomon of old. Then Jesus tells us that we are of more value than many birds and that even the hairs of our head are numbered because God knows us inside out. He reminds us that God is the one who created us and loves us unconditionally. In fact, he creates us to be absolutely unique. No two of us are the same! When God created you and me he threw out the mold. Long ago God said something to the prophet Jeremiah that he says to you and me, "Before I formed you in the womb I knew you, and before you were born I consecrated you ..." (Jeremiah 1:5).

If you and I were an idea in the mind of God *before* we were formed in the womb then we are created for a plan and purpose. God puts dreams into our hearts that he wants us to grab a hold of and fulfill. Such knowledge adds purpose and meaning to our existence and can give us a sense of peace. We can know beyond all doubt that we are loved and cared for by the God who created us for his plans, and this knowledge can give us the realization that the real antidote for anxieties and fears lies in gratitude. Gratitude and thanksgiving are the opposite of self-centeredness and bitterness. Real thanksgiving comes out of our faith and results in joy, hope, and peace.

When the Apostle Paul was in a prison cell waiting to be executed, he wrote a letter to one of the congregations he had helped to establish in Philippi, Greece. In this letter, written in a drafty, cold prison full of the specter of death, he writes: "Do not worry about anything, but in everything by prayer and supplication with thanksgiving let your requests be made known to God. And the peace of God which surpasses all understanding will guard your hearts and minds in Christ Jesus" (Philippians 4:6-7).

Pastor Charles Allen tells of a meaningful Thanksgiving worship service in which he was really blessed. He looked out over the congregation and saw sitting near the front a couple who had lost their son in the war in Korea. Then in a few rows behind them he saw a certain woman who had desired all her life to be a wife and mother, but her parents became ill when she was young and she had devoted her life to taking care of them. Although oftentimes lonely, she never gave in to self-pity. In the back of the church he noticed a man who had been in and out of jail. He had grown up in the streets, poor and unloved. All these people were dealing with their own private heartaches and anxieties and fears. Each one of them was there in church that day singing thanks to God.[9]

The older I become, the more I realize that peace is not some kind of static and unemotional concept. It is a powerful moving force that is like a flowing river. This flowing peace within us produces the courage to act in decisive ways. The real secret of being more alive than ever is this inner sense of peace that gives us the energy to cope with a myriad of problems no matter how severe.

Maybe you know the story of Olympic speed skating champion, Dan Janson. Dan was the favorite in the 1988 Calgary Olympics. Just before he was to race he was given the message that his sister Jane's long battle against leukemia had ended in death. "When I finally got on the ice for the 500-meter race," writes Dan in his autobiography, *Full Circle*, "I felt wobbly as if I hadn't been on skates in six months." He thought of Jane, "Jane is dead. Should I be here? How can my parents cheer for me while facing the burial of a child? Jane's dead." Unable to concentrate, Janson had a terrible Olympics. His performance was compounded by his guilt. "You jerk," he thought, "your sister just died." His lack of success at skating should not matter to him under such circumstances, he thought, but it did.

Things did not improve much for Dan in the 1992 Olympics. In spite of a history of winning some championships he was becoming an athlete who "chokes" when his biggest test of all comes. He retained the services of a sports psychologist. Yet no matter what he did or tried his performance at skating was full of slips and falls.

How well I remember the 1,000-meter race in the 1992 Olympics. I sat glued to the television and felt I was sitting on pins and needles. Janson had never won this event before and this was probably his last chance ever to win a gold medal. Approaching the starting line he touched a ring around his neck containing the birthstone of his eight-month daughter, Jane, named after his late sister. To our dismay, once more, in a major race, Dan slipped, but this time he did not falter as he had before and when he crossed the finish line first, the noise was deafening. Dan Janson finally won his gold medal in the Olympics, and the victory was won on the ice only after it was won in his own heart and mind. The inward storms of guilt and fears, anxieties, and worries were overcome by an inward sense of peace that could only have come through the God of peace. This peace flowed like a river through his being and gave him an inward strength and discipline and courage that enabled him to be more alive than ever.

Like the great storms that came across the prairies, there are storms that come into your life and mine. The winds of problems and cares are ever-shifting and moving in all directions. Our sense of peace can become precarious indeed. But the God who loves us in Jesus can say to us again, "Peace, be still." This Jesus comes to us in the midst of the storm and says, "It is I, do not be afraid." We can know again that nothing, absolutely nothing can separate us from his loving care. Inward peace is a precious gift that can enable us to be more alive than ever.

Reflection And Discussion

Thought Questions

1. What kind of danger threatened the disciples of Jesus?

2. Why are the disciples filled with terror?

3. How was the terror overcome?

4. In what different ways does Jesus come to us today?

Agree Or Disagree

- Fear keeps us from doing what we should do.

- God does not always protect us.

- Everyone who prays escapes from danger and experiences peace.

Endnotes

1. Sami Awwad, *The Holy Land In Color* (Jerusalem: Polphot Ltd.). (This book is revised and updated frequently.)

2. William Barclay, *The New Daily Study Bible, The Gospel of John*, Vol. 1 (Louisville/ London: Westminster John Knox Press, 1995, 2001), pp. 241-245.

3. William Barclay, *The Daily Study Bible, The Gospel of Matthew*, Vol. 1 (Philadelphia: The Westminster Press, 1956, 1958), pp. 322-323.

4. Sherwood E. Wirt, *Jesus, Man of Joy* (Eugene, Oregon: Harvest House Publications, 1999), pp. 17-18, 61ff.

5. Georgia Witkin, *The Female Stress Survival Guide* (New York: Newmarket Press, 2002).

6. Georgia Witkin, *The Male Stress Survival Guide* (New York: Newmarket Press, 2003), Witkin books quoted in *East Valley Tribune*, Mesa, Arizona, February 27, 2003.

7. The 10 most stressful events from Thomas H. Holmes and Richard H. Roche, "The Social Readjustment Rating Scale" — Journal of Psychosomatic Research.

8. David B. Wilhelm, M.D., *RX For The Soul* (Nashville: Thomas Nelson Publishers, 1997), pp. 24-30.

9. Charles L. Allen, *God's 7 Wonders For You* (Old Tappan, New Jersey: Fleming H. Revell Company, 1987), pp. 48-49.

Other Resources

Gerald Sloyan, *Interpretation — John* (Atlanta: John Knox Press, 1988), pp. 66-67.

Denis Waitley, *Ten Seeds Of Greatness* (Old Tappan, New Jersey: Fleming H. Revell Company, 1983), pp. 172-185.

Robert Kysar, *Augsburg Commentary on the New Testament — John* (Minneapolis: Augsburg Publishing House, 1986), pp. 93-96.

Bonnie St. John Deane, *Succeeding Sane* (New York: Simon & Schuster, 1998), p. 168.

The Sixth Sign — *John 9:1-41*

Seeing Is Getting The Mud Out Of Your Eyes

As he walked along, he saw a man blind from birth. His disciples asked him, "Rabbi, who sinned, this man or his parents, that he was born blind?" Jesus answered, "Neither this man nor his parents sinned; he was born blind so that God's works might be revealed in him. We must work the works of him who sent me while it is day; night is coming when no one can work. As long as I am in the world, I am the light of the world." When he had said this, he spat on the ground and made mud with the saliva and spread the mud on the man's eyes, saying to him, "Go, wash in the pool of Siloam" (which means Sent). Then he went and washed and came back able to see. The neighbors and those who had seen him before as a beggar began to ask, "Is this not the man who used to sit and beg?" Some were saying, "It is he." Others were saying, "No, but it is someone like him." He kept saying, "I am the man." But they kept asking him, "Then how were your eyes opened?" He answered, "The man called Jesus made mud, spread it on my eyes, and said to me, 'Go to Siloam and wash.' Then I went and washed and received my sight." They said to him, "Where is he?" He said, "I do not know."

They brought to the Pharisees the man who had formerly been blind. Now it was a sabbath day when Jesus made the mud and opened his eyes. Then the Pharisees also began to ask him how he had received his sight. He said to them, "He put mud on my eyes. Then I washed, and now I see." Some of the Pharisees said, "This man is not from God, for he does not observe the sabbath." But others said, "How can a man who is a sinner perform such signs?" And they were divided. So they said again to the blind man, "What do you say about him? It was your eyes he opened." He said, "He is a prophet."

The Jews did not believe that he had been blind and had received his sight until they called the parents of the man who had received his sight and asked them, "Is this your son, who you say was born blind? How then does he now see?" His parents answered, "We know that this is our son, and that he was born blind; but we do not know how it is that now he sees, nor do we know who opened his eyes. Ask him; he is of age. He will speak for himself." His parents said this because they were afraid of the Jews; for the Jews had already agreed that anyone who confessed Jesus to be the Messiah would be put out of the synagogue. Therefore his parents said, "He is of age; ask him."

So for the second time they called the man who had been blind, and they said to him, "Give glory to God! We know that this man is a sinner." He answered, "I do not know whether he is a sinner. One thing I do know, that though I was blind, now I see." They said to him, "What did he do to you? How did he open your eyes?" He answered them, "I have told you already, and you would not listen. Why do you want to hear it again? Do you also want to become his disciples?" Then they reviled him, saying, "You are his disciple, but we are disciples of Moses. We know that God has spoken to Moses, but as for this man, we do not know where he comes from." The man answered, "Here is an astonishing thing! You do not know where he comes from, and yet he opened my eyes. We know that God does not listen to sinners, but he does listen to one who worships him and obeys his will. Never since the world began has it been heard that anyone opened the eyes of a person born blind. If this man were not from God, he could do nothing." They answered him, "You were born entirely in sins, and are you trying to teach us?" And they drove him out.

Jesus heard that they had driven him out, and when he found him, he said, "Do you believe in the Son of

Man?" He answered, "And who is he, sir? Tell me, so that I may believe in him." Jesus said to him, "You have seen him, and the one speaking with you is he." He said, "Lord, I believe." And he worshiped him. Jesus said, "I came into this world for judgment so that those who do not see may see, and those who do see may become blind." Some of the Pharisees near him heard this and said to him, "Surely we are not blind, are we?" Jesus said to them, "If you were blind, you would not have sin. But now that you say, 'We see,' your sin remains."

The Lord giveth sight to the blind.
— *Prayer Book*, Church of England, 1662

    The sixth sign and miracle is the restoration of sight to a man born blind. Along with the gift of physical sight there came an increasing spiritual insight and sight. The blind man in his relationship to Jesus received the gift of a growing and dynamic faith. The mud was truly washed out of his eyes and he received new wisdom and understanding. He received the courage to witness to his faith and became wondrously alive.

    Once I had an associate pastor whose wife, Susan, was born blind. She was a beautiful woman with a strong faith and marvelous spirit, and how she could sing. Hers was one of those golden voices with great range that could lift and inspire the listener. To me she had the voice of an angel, and Susan could "see" in many ways. During the coffee hour between our Sunday worship services I would often sit down and converse with Susan. One day I discovered she was a Minnesota Viking football fan and she proceeded to talk about the game that had taken place on the previous Sunday. In fact, she described the game in such vivid detail that I forgot for a moment that she was blind.

    My wife, Judy, and Susan became good friends and often sat together toward the front of the worship center. As I led the morning worship I noticed the two of them were laughing so hard that both of them were shaking. Later, I discovered that Judy had said to Susan that she was having trouble singing the hymns because she had forgotten her glasses. Susan promptly replied, "So you think you have problems seeing!"

Susan, though blind, had a sparkling sense of humor. Not only that, she could see and sense the people around her in remarkable ways. How often before the worship people would come up to Judy and talk to her and greet her in the narthex not saying anything to Susan standing next to her. It was almost as if they didn't see or notice her because she was blind. Perhaps they were uncomfortable because they were not used to being around the blind, but Susan felt their presence and noticed them. At times it was as if she could see and feel the personalities and dress of those around her. One day she said to Judy, "That woman is dressed kind of dowdy today, isn't she?"

In the Gospel of John our attention is focused upon a man born blind. Obviously he was a well-known character and beggar in the streets of Jerusalem. Even the disciples of Jesus knew who he was. One day when the blind man was coming down the street the disciples raised the question as to whether the man's blindness was a result of his sins or the sins of his parents. To their way of thinking there was a close relationship between blindness and sin. If a person lived a sinful life it would result in sicknesses and accidents. According to the book of Exodus the sins of the parents had an affect upon the children. The writer pictures the Lord God as saying, "I the Lord your God am a jealous God, punishing children for the iniquity of parents, to the third and the fourth generation of those who reject me, but showing steadfast love to the thousandth generation of those who love me and keep my commandments" (Exodus 20:5-6). Jesus was quick to answer, "Neither this man nor his parents sinned; he was born blind so that God's works might be revealed in him" (John 9:3).[1]

This is the setting of the sixth sign or miracle through which we can catch sight and insight into what it really means to be able to see. The miracle before us lets us know that there are two kinds of blindness, physical and spiritual. There can be blindness in our eyes, and blindness in our minds and spirits. There can be an inward blindness that can affect what we see or don't see. There can be an inward blindness that can keep us from the abundant life Jesus wants us to have.

Back in 1991, there was an article in the *New York Times* magazine concerning a group of more than one hundred women who lived in Long Beach, California. These women were Cambodian refugees who witnessed the horror and tortures of the Pol Pot Regime. They were declared certifiably blind even though doctors said their eyes functioned perfectly well. These women suffered from psychosomatic or hysterical blindness. They were really blind, but their blindness stemmed from their minds.

Of course psychosomatic disorders are nothing new. We know that the state of our minds can affect our speech, our hearing, and our memory, as well as our sight. It is said that scientists really do not understand this phenomenon, only that it shows the power of the mind over the body. One researcher attempted to explain the refugees' disorder as follows: "Losing eyesight makes sense if you are trying to escape the stress of a situation. At the movie theater you don't cover your ears when grotesque and loud violence comes on the screen. You'll always cover your eyes."[2]

Recently there came to my attention a phenomenon called "blindsight." Studies show that certain blind people have become sightless as a result of stroke or brain injury, rather than damage to the eye, and some of these people do a remarkable thing. If an object is put in front of them and if they are asked to reach for the object, they will say it is impossible, since they cannot see it. But if they are persuaded to try, they will find the object with a certainty that amazes even themselves. This uncanny ability is called "blindsight." Anthony Marcel, a psychologist at Cambridge University, who has done research on "blindsight" states that "these people theoretically have superb vision, but they don't know they can see. The brain damage that has rendered these patients blind is not in those areas that have to do with seeing. Technically their vision is fine. What their eyes see, however, is never transmitted to the part of the brain that brings vision into awareness. They can see — they just don't know it."[3]

Now we return to the gospel story. Jesus is aware of blindness. He knows that blindness is caused by many things. He knows that blindness can be a channel of healing not just for the eyes but for the mind and spirit and heart. It is Jesus who reaches out to the blind man. It is Jesus who wants this man not only to see physically but spiritually as well. He spits upon the ground and makes some mud and packs it into his eyes and tells him to go and wash out his eyes in the pool of Siloam located within the walls of the city of Jerusalem. This pool of water came from the Gihon Spring outside the city walls and flowed through a tunnel that was dug through solid rock centuries before during the days of Hezekiah. Siloam means "sent" and refers to the water sent through the tunnel into the heart of the city. When one thinks of this pool of water it is easy to think of Jesus as the water of life sent to us to reach out to our blindness that keeps us from being more alive than ever.[4]

Now we look upon an amazing sight. A blind man stumbling along with mud in his eyes being led by his friends through the streets and down into the pool of Siloam. When he washes out his eyes he can see! He must have run through the streets shouting, "I can see! I can see!" No question about it. This miracle of sight began to stir the whole city.

James L. Kraft, a renowned Christian layperson, recalls as a great turning point in his life the day that he met a certain kindly eye doctor. James was a fourteen-year-old boy, one of a family of eleven children, living on a farm in Canada. In his book, *Adventure in Jade*, he relates that he had never been able to distinguish objects clearly. His nearsightedness was so acute and so distressing that he assumed everyone on earth suffered continuously from furious headaches, and that all the earth had the blurry image of a boat seen from under water. One summer an eye doctor from the city was vacationing in the vicinity, and young James was taking care of the doctor's horse and buggy. Noting his extreme nearsightedness, the eye doctor insisted that James go to the city with him to be fitted with a pair of glasses. In that gift of glasses Kraft gratefully recalls, "He gave me the earth and all that was in it, completely in focus and beautiful beyond anything I could have dreamed ... I cannot think of another act of human kindness," Kraft concludes, "in my lifetime which can compare with that of the good doctor."[5]

Jesus not only healed the blind man but sought him out. Some years ago there was a great revival that spread across America. There was a remarkable turning back to God and return to the churches, similar to what happened following the attack upon and destruction of the Twin Towers by the terrorists. In evangelism services people began to speak of finding Jesus. There were even bumper stickers on many cars that said, "I Found Him!" Then I began to notice more and more bumper stickers that said, "Jesus Found Me!" It was true with the blind man and it is true with us today. Jesus has sought and is seeking us out to give us new sight and insight into what we can become. Jesus comes to make us more alive than ever. He comes to give us new abilities to see outwardly and inwardly so that the world around us is more in focus and more beautiful beyond anything we could have dreamed. Some time ago I wrote a little verse that has become a daily prayer in my life, and it can be yours as well: "I'm looking for you Jesus, O find me now today, and lift me on the high road, to walk along your way. Jesus Savior be forever near me. And let me hear you say, Lord, 'Come abide with me.'"

When you read the rest of the ninth chapter of John you discover that when the blind man could see again, it affected many people. It certainly affected the parents who were afraid of the Pharisees. It affected the crowds who more and more believed in Jesus as a prophet from God because he healed the sick and caused the blind to see. It affected the Pharisees who wanted to get rid of Jesus since he had broken the law by healing on the Sabbath. They wondered what was wrong with this Jesus. He could have healed a man born blind on any other day except the Sabbath. To their way of thinking it was an open defiance of the laws. Such a one could not be the Messiah that was to come. Yet even some of the Pharisees had mixed feelings. The healed blind man was a walking miracle that everyone could see. Anyone who could heal a man born blind must be from God.

The blind man who could now see affected his friends and neighbors. They could hardly believe that this man was the former beggar in the streets. If you who are reading this were born blind and suddenly were able to see, you would be different. You would walk differently. Your appearance would change. The way you talked would be more animated and direct. Your whole mind and spirit and actions would be different. You might even run through the streets shouting, "I can see! I can see!"

Yet many people who have physical eyes that can see are blind in many ways. We can have mud in our eyes that keeps us from the sight and insight necessary to really be able to see. Prejudice of any kind is like mud. So is anger and hatred. Ignorance is like mud producing darkness that can keep us from seeing what we should see. The lack of visions and dreams is a mud that keeps us from seeing what we can do and what we can be. Anxiety and worry and stresses of life are like a mud producing blindness that keeps us from being focused on today and the present moment and the opportunity to serve. And Jesus sees us stumbling along. He comes to us. He finds us. He asks us to wash our eyes in his water of life, so that we can see him and his power. And when we can see clearly again, we will know him as our Lord and Savior. We become more alive than ever.

The man born blind was able to see physically and then slowly, but surely, began to see spiritually. Like the dawning of a new day he began to realize who Jesus was. In his first conversation with the Pharisees he spoke of the one who healed him as the man called Jesus. Later on he said to them that Jesus was a prophet since only a prophet could enable a man born blind to see. In fact, he went so far as to say, "Never since the world began has it been heard that anyone opened the eyes of a person born blind. If this man were not from God, he could do nothing" (John 9:32-33). The Pharisees were so angered by his words that they drove him away.

Though now isolated in many ways from his parents, his neighbors, and friends this man continued to search for the truth. He longed for an abundant more fulfilling life. Well, wonder of wonders, Jesus sought him out again. He spoke and reasoned with him. Suddenly there came to him through the words of Jesus the conviction that Jesus was the Son of God sent into the world. We are told quite clearly that he exclaimed to Jesus, "Lord, I believe," and that then he worshiped him (John 9:38). Now he could really see and he became wonderfully alive.

Helen Keller is the name of a woman who not only was born blind but also deaf. She once wrote, "I learned that it is possible for us to create light, sound, and order no matter what calamity may befall us in the outer world."[6] Blindness in need of light is such a part of life, even for the very young. As I write this there is, in our state of Iowa, a seven-year-old girl who can see the light. Her name is Annabelle Costanzo. She was born fifteen weeks premature in July, 1996. She was diagnosed with retinopathy of the eyes, a condition in babies born when their eyes are still developing. Sight improves for many children born with the condition, but in Annabelle's case, it caused rapid blindness.

Early on, Annabelle's parents, Nick and Gina Costanzo, designed a light box made with a light that could be turned on and off and it mesmerized Annabelle for a period of three years when she had some limited vision. Then for the last four years she has been completely blind and the light box was put away into storage. Just recently Annabelle underwent eye surgery in Detroit. Her doctor, Michael Trese, said it might allow her to see some light and, possibly, color. After Annabelle came home the parents pulled the light box out of storage. Annabelle pressed her face to the top of the box in the family's darkened basement, as her mother slowly and quietly adjusted a dial on the side.

"Is it on or off?" Gina Costanzo asked when the light was turned on as high as it would go.

"On," Annabelle said.

Gina flipped off the light.

"Off," Annabelle said immediately, tapping her fingers excitedly against the plastic top.

The room erupted in applause.

Annabelle beamed.

It was the first time in four years the girl had detected light. While her family was elated that Annabelle could see the light, there was no indication that she could see colors. Placing blue and red slides on the light produced no reaction, and a flashing, multicolored disco ball did not appear to register in Annabelle's eyes.

Annabelle is likely to require many more surgeries before her sight is noticeably improved. Seeing the light is a first step toward what they hope will be a greater range of sight someday, her parents said.[7]

Now seeing and experiencing the light of Jesus is important to really being able to see opportunities to serve outwardly and greater truths inwardly, even if one is physically blind. Robert Schuller tells the story of Stanley Krawczyk who was 21 years old when he had an accident which left him blind. Yet his faith and a sense of humor carried him through. Eventually Stanley became a dynamic leader in his community. Stanley had such a zest for fun that it became a driving force to bring some levity into the lives of those who were dreary and depressed. He began to plan parties at the local hospital. Every month he rounded up ninety volunteers, hired an orchestra, and gave the patients the best time of their lives.

Next Stanley put his talents to work in a children's home where he planned picnics with ice cream, pop machines, hot dogs, and an orchestra. All they could eat for free! Over 100 children enjoyed the picnic thanks to Stanley. He also raised $5,000 to construct a shelter for outside activities. Then he planned parties and dances for a retirement home and again, the food was all free.

Stanley laughs as he tells about the time he was called by the American Cancer Society. They asked if he would be willing to drive people to the hospital, and Stanley did not let on that he was blind. Instead he called around and found someone to drive. For two years he and his friends drove patients to their appointments. One day Stanley had a heart attack and wasn't able to do his volunteer work anymore. It was then that the people of the Cancer Society discovered that their reliable driver was blind!

Life has been full for Stanley Krawczyk. He has brought laughter and fun into lives that would have known nothing but despair. Not only have patients' lives been touched, but also all the volunteers that he has ministered to through the years.

After forty years of helping people, Stanley says, "I count my blessings and thank God for allowing me to go blind. It was very difficult at first ... but I wouldn't have lived the life I've lived had

I not been blind. One can be blind in his eyes but that doesn't make him blind in his heart."[8]

With Helen Keller, Stanley, and Annabelle, and a mighty host of others, we can know that there are two kinds of blindness — the blindness of the eyes and the blindness of the heart. Jesus our Lord, alive today, comes to us and finds us! He seeks to bring us to the light. With his wonderful, immeasurable water of life he can wash the mud out of our eyes and makes us more alive than ever.

Reflection And Discussion

Thought Questions

1. Why does Jesus say that the man was born blind?

2. What steps did the man have to take to receive his sight? Why?

3. Why were the Pharisees so angry at Jesus for healing a blind man?

4. How do you think you would feel if you were the parents of the man born blind?

Agree Or Disagree

- It is important to come to Jesus and ask in order to receive healing power.

- All sickness and disease are a result of sin.

Endnotes

1. William Barclay, *The New Daily Bible Study, The Gospel of John*, Vol. 2 (Louisville: Westminster John Knox Press, 1975), pp. 37-52.

2. "They Cried Until They Could Not See" — Patrick Cooke, Vol. 140, *New York Times* magazine, June 23, 1991, p. 24, et seg.

3. Daniel Goleman, Ph.D., *Vital Lies Simple Truths* (New York: Simon & Schuster, 1985).

4. *Op. cit.*, Barclay.

5. Leo Buscalgia, *Bus 9 to Paradise* (New York: Slack, Inc., 1986), p. 51.

6. "Annabelle" story from *The Des Moines Register*, November 4, 2003.

7. *Ibid.*

8. Robert H. Schuller, *Life's Not Fair But God is Good* (Nashville: Thomas Nelson Publishers, 1991), pp. 153-157.

Other Resources

V. Eugene Johnson, *The Seven Signs in the Gospel of John* (Rock Island, Illinois: Augustana Book Concern, 1955), pp. 52-60.

Roger L. Fredrikson (Lloyd J. Ogilvie, General Editor), *The Communicator's Commentary — John*, Vol. 4 (Waco, Texas: Word Books, 1985), pp. 167-178.

The Seventh Sign — *John 11:1-44*

New Life Is Like A Grain Of Wheat

Now a certain man was ill, Lazarus of Bethany, the village of Mary and her sister Martha. Mary was the one who anointed the Lord with perfume and wiped his feet with her hair; her brother Lazarus was ill. So the sisters sent a message to Jesus, "Lord, he whom you love is ill." But when Jesus heard it, he said, "This illness does not lead to death; rather it is for God's glory, so that the Son of God may be glorified through it." Accordingly, though Jesus loved Martha and her sister and Lazarus, after having heard that Lazarus was ill, he stayed two days longer in the place where he was.

Then after this he said to the disciples, "Let us go to Judea again." The disciples said to him, "Rabbi, the Jews were just now trying to stone you, and are you going there again?" Jesus answered, "Are there not twelve hours of daylight? Those who walk during the day do not stumble, because they see the light of this world. But those who walk at night stumble, because the light is not in them." After saying this, he told them, "Our friend Lazarus has fallen asleep, but I am going there to awaken him." The disciples said to him, "Lord, if he has fallen asleep, he will be all right." Jesus, however, had been speaking about his death, but they thought that he was referring merely to sleep. Then Jesus told them plainly, "Lazarus is dead. For your sake I am glad I was not there, so that you may believe. But let us go to him." Thomas, who was called the Twin, said to his fellow disciples, "Let us also go, that we may die with him."

When Jesus arrived, he found that Lazarus had already been in the tomb four days. Now Bethany was near Jerusalem, some two miles away, and many of the Jews had come to Martha and Mary to console them about their brother. When Martha heard that Jesus was coming, she went and met him, while Mary stayed at home. Martha said to Jesus, "Lord, if you had been here, my brother would not have died. But even now I know that God will give you whatever you ask of him." Jesus said to her, "Your brother will rise again." Martha said to him, "I know that he will rise again in the resurrection on the last day." Jesus said to him, "I am the resurrection and the life. Those who believe in me, even though they die, will live, and everyone who lives and believes in me will never die. Do you believe this?" She said to him, "Yes, Lord, I believe that you are the Messiah, the Son of God, the one coming into the world."

When she had said this, she went back and called her sister Mary, and told her privately, "The Teacher is here and is calling for you." And when she heard it, she got up quickly and went to him. Now Jesus had not yet come to the village, but was still at the place where Martha had met him. The Jews who were with her in the house, consoling her, saw Mary get up quickly and go out. They followed her because they thought that she was going to the tomb to weep there. When Mary came where Jesus was and saw him, she knelt at his feet and said to him, "Lord, if you had been here, my brother would not have died." When Jesus saw her weeping, and the Jews who came with her also weeping, he was greatly disturbed in spirit and deeply moved. He said, "Where have you laid him?" They said to him, "Lord, come and see." Jesus began to weep. So the Jews said, "See how he loved him!" But some of them said, "Could not he who opened the eyes of the blind man kept this man from dying?"

Then Jesus, again greatly disturbed, came to the tomb. It was a cave, and a stone was lying against it. Jesus said, "Take away the stone." Martha, the sister of the dead man, said to him, "Lord, already there is a stench because he has been dead four days." Jesus said to her, "Did I not tell you that if you believed you would see the glory of God?" So they took away the *stone. And Jesus looked upward and said, "Father, I thank you for having heard me. I knew that you always hear me, but I have said this for the sake of the crowd standing here, so that they may believe that you sent me." When he had said this, he cried with a loud voice, "Lazarus, come out!" The dead man came out, his hands and feet bound with strips of cloth, and his face wrapped in a cloth. Jesus said to them, "Unbind him, and let him go."*

> *Grow old along with me!*
> *The best is yet to be.*
> — Browning

We look now into the seventh sign, the sign of new life. In the resurrection of Lazarus from the dead there came a new life to his family and friends and to many in the Jerusalem area. We, too, can know again that not even death can separate us from the love of God. Once more there can be the trumpet sounds of victory and new life.

There is an old story about a man who decided one Saturday to clean the basement. In one corner was an old desk that contained some old files and various drawers full of old, discarded things. To his amazement he discovered an old shoe ticket that should have been used to pick up a pair of shoes he had taken in for repair months before. Why he had forgotten all about them! He wondered if the repair shop still had the shoes. So he went down and went into the shop and presented the shoe ticket and asked, "Do you by any chance still have these shoes?" The man took the ticket and was gone for a few moments and then came back and said, "Yes the shoes are here, and they will be ready next Monday!"

Just a silly old story, but it certainly could be true since we often are a people who procrastinate when it comes to getting something done. We remind ourselves that the time to become more alive than ever is today. It is this moment that we can turn to Jesus and the power of his Spirit among us. It is right now as you read this that you can remember again the channels of a life force that can enable us to be more alive than ever.

When John wrote his gospel we are reminded again that he chose only seven of the many miracles of Jesus which he calls "signs." The author is very selective for a reason. There were, of course, many other miracles and things that Jesus said and did causing the author to write, "but *these* are written so that you may come to believe that Jesus is the Messiah, the Son of God, and that through believing you may have life in his name" (John 20:21). In each of these miracles or signs there is a remarkable quality of life that enables us to be more alive than ever.

There is the *joy* of the wedding feast in Cana where Jesus turned water into wine. This sparkling, refreshing joy can be cultivated in our lives each day. If you have not done it yet run to the mirror right now and practice letting out the biggest belly laugh you can manufacture. Not only will it be good exercise, it will open you up to the quality of joy.

There is the *trust* of the royal official who had journeyed for over a day from Capernaum to Cana to find Jesus and to ask him to come and heal his young son who was close to death. But the official had to return alone without Jesus, trusting only in his command, "Go; your son will live" (John 4:50). This quality of trust is like a sheltering umbrella in a world that rains down upon us disappointments and discouragements.

And there is the quality of *hope* that can come to us when we are like the paralyzed man beside the pool of Bethzatha in Jerusalem. A man who was so discouraged and helpless after being ill for 38 years that he couldn't move until Jesus came along and said, "Stand, take up your mat and walk" (John 5:8). This quality of hope can enable us to come alive and perform actions of mercy to ourselves and those around us.

Then we are confronted with a miracle that is so important that it is the only miracle found in all the four gospels. It is the historical account of Jesus feeding a crowd of thousands with a little boy's lunch of five barley loaves and two little fishes. Jesus made this claim: "I am the bread of life. Whoever comes to me will never be hungry, and whoever believes in me will never be thirsty" (John 6:35). Yes, there is the *bread* and *nourishment* of the presence of Jesus and his words in our lives and spirits that make us more alive than ever, and this bread is a special nourishing force that energizes us and inspires us to serve others.

In the midst of the storms of life there is the inward *peace* that passes all understanding that Jesus places in our hearts as he walks on the stormy waves into our lives. There is the *sight* and *insight* that comes from the Jesus who restored the sight of a man born blind. Getting close to Jesus provides counsel and light, understanding and wisdom that gets the mud out of our eyes, enabling us to see the direction we are to take this and every day.

We look now upon a final quality that can enable us to be more alive than ever. When we moved to a new parish in Olivia, Minnesota, we inherited a newly built church and education wing located on the southwest corner of the town next to Highway 71 and the open country. Here was a beautiful setting in the midst of rolling wooded hills surrounded by fields of corn and beans. The church was all completed except for the windows in the worship center that were to be made of frosted glass. One day a widow donated a substantial sum of money as a memorial to her husband who had been a great leader and pillar of strength in the congregation. It was specifically designated for new stained glass windows. After much study and research we found an artist who had a huge stained glass studio in his home in Saint Paul. We loved the work he had done, so he was commissioned by the congregation to do the new windows. They were to be designed to show the key events in the life of Jesus from his birth to his death and resurrection. The window showing the resurrection contained a unique design that had grains of wheat. We were all given some new insight into the teachings of Jesus concerning his death and resurrection when the artist explained to us that the window reflected the words of Jesus when he said, "The hour has come for the Son of Man to be glorified. Very truly, I tell you, unless a grain of wheat falls into the earth and dies, it remains just a single grain; but if it dies, it bears much fruit" (John 12:23b-24). In our own personal lives there often needs to be the death of old habits and old ways of doing things for new life to develop. Jesus was right. The farmers around Olivia who were members of the congregation of course knew that when a seed is placed into the ground it didn't really die, it germinated. It experienced an explosion of *new growth*. They knew that Jesus was right in a symbolical way and that this kind of growth can happen to you and me.

Often on a Sunday afternoon I would sit in the worship center in the quietness alone and meditate upon the life of Jesus with the sunlight filtering through the stained glass windows. How they showed the life of Jesus from his birth to his suffering and dying and to the resurrection and new life with marvelous symbols, especially those simple grains of wheat. There would come again to one's heart and mind those words of Jesus, "I came that you may have life, and have it abundantly." Yes, new life comes so often out of the dying experiences of life. When a person, for example, overcomes an all-consuming destructive addiction there is the death of an old life and the emergence of a new. The quality of new, abundant, overflowing life overcomes the old. And yes, my friends, when physical death comes there is a new life that follows.

We look now into the final sign and miracle. Jesus in his ministry had a home away from home. Every time he would come to the city of Jerusalem he would stay in the village of Bethany. This little town was located two miles across the Kidron Valley from Jerusalem. How well I remember going to Bethany and looking across the valley at a simply magnificent view of the old city with the Dome of the Rock dominating the old site of the temple. In a beautiful garden setting in Bethany today a church marks the site of the sign and miracle before us. In Bethany in the days of Jesus lived a man called Lazarus with his sisters, Mary and Martha. This home was a source of love, strength, protection, and comfort for Jesus.

When I was in the ninth grade the grandmother who raised my sister and me moved to Poulsbo, Washington, located across Puget Sound from Seattle and about seventeen miles north of Bremerton. Here was a beautiful town that was built in layers moving up into the pine covered hills up from the bay on which the town was situated. The whole area was surrounded by mountains, the Olympics on one side and the Cascades on the other. We lived on the edge of town by a small piece of open country nestled in among the wooded hills. Often on a Sunday afternoon my sister and I and our friends would play in the open field and hike through the woods. Once in the late fall as we were hiking through the forest the weather changed dramatically. The temperature dropped quickly and a cold misty rain began to fall. We were chilled to the bone and shivering when we finally walked out of the woods into the open field. Darkness had begun to descend and as we looked through the misty, rainy fog we could make out the outline of our home with a lighted window. It promised warmth, food, and loving comfort, and we ran through the field. That picture of warmth of a lighted window in the growing dusk always comes to mind when I think of the home in Bethany. Here was a place of refuge in the midst of the growing storm of suffering and death that surrounded Jesus.

One day there came a message to Jesus and his disciples that Lazarus was very sick and close to death. Surprisingly Jesus doesn't immediately travel to Bethany. He delays and says to the disciples, "This illness does not lead to death; rather it is for God's glory, so that the Son of God may be glorified through it" (John 11:4). As the story unfolds one can relate to Mary and Martha who waited and waited for Jesus to come. Waiting is such a part of life. At the University of Wisconsin a study was done on how we spend our time. It was calculated that during an average seventy-year lifetime we spend twenty years working, twenty years sleeping, seven years in sports and recreation, nine months in putting on and taking off shoes, and three years in waiting for someone or something!

We wait and wait most every day. How we wait for doctors and healing power. Doctors are so busy and overloaded with patients. As someone said, more and more of them are running their practices like an assembly line. There is an old story about a fellow who walked into a doctor's office and the receptionist asked him what he had. He promptly replied, "Shingles." She took down his name, address, medical insurance number, and told him to have a seat. Fifteen minutes later a nurse's aide came over and asked him what he had. Again he replied, "Shingles." She took down his height, weight, a complete medical history, and told him to wait in an examining room. About twenty minutes later a nurse came in and asked what he had and again he said, "Shingles." She gave him a blood test took his temperature and blood pressure. Then she told him to take off his shirt and wait for the doctor. Some time later the doctor came in and said, "I understand you have shingles. Where do you have them?" He replied, "Outside in the truck, where do want them?"

According to the American Medical Association, the leading complaint of Americans about doctors is the time it takes waiting for them. It is frustrating to be feeling terrible and then have to wait. It's even worse when we're concerned about someone we love. And so Mary and Martha waited and waited for Jesus. By the time he arrived, Lazarus had died and had been buried in a cave for four days. If you and I had a loved one who had died while we waited for the doctor to come for days we would not only be outraged but would probably sue the hospital and the medical profession.

But this story is dealing not just with a family in crisis. It is dealing with a world full of suffering due to sin and death. It is a story of life and death and life again. It is given to us to show us that Jesus is the author of new life, yes, even the author of new life beyond death. It is to show us that Jesus is the resurrection and the life. And it is this God through Jesus who comes to us in the valleys of sorrow and death in his own time and in his own way.

When Jesus came to Bethany, Lazarus had been dead for four days and buried in a cave in the nearby cemetery. The whole scene is filled with deep emotions and feelings. William Barclay, in his writings, visualizes the scene of a funeral for us:

> *As many as possible attended a funeral. Everyone who could was supposed, in courtesy and respect, to join the procession on its way. One curious custom was that the women walked first, for it was held that since woman by her first sin brought death into the world, she ought to lead the mourners to the tomb. At the tomb memorial speeches were sometimes made. Everyone was expected to express the deepest sympathy, and, on leaving the tomb, the others stood in two long lines*

while the principal mourners passed between them. But there was this very wise rule — the mourners were not to be tormented by idle and uninvited talk. They were to be left, at that moment, alone with their sorrow.

In the house of mourning there were set customs. So long as the body was in the house it was forbidden to eat meat or to drink wine, to wear phylacteries or to engage in any kind of study. No food was to be prepared in the house, and such food as was eaten must not be eaten in the presence of the dead. As soon as the body was carried out all furniture was reversed, and the mourners sat on the ground or on low stools.

Deep mourning lasted for seven days, of which the first three were days of weeping. During these seven days it was forbidden to anoint oneself, to put on shoes, to engage in any kind of study or business, and even to wash. The week of deep mourning was followed by thirty days of lighter mourning.[2]

It was to such a scene of mourning that Jesus came. When Martha heard that Jesus was approaching Bethany she went running out to meet him. Her first words to Jesus seem very understandable under the circumstances. "Lord, if you had been here my brother would not have died." Jesus assured her saying, "Your brother will rise again." Martha agreed with Jesus thinking that this would be true on the last day way in the future. Then Jesus spoke the words that are expressed over and over in Christian funerals today. "I am the resurrection and the life. Those who believe in me, even though they die, will live, and whoever lives and believes in me will never die." Martha replied, "Yes, Lord, I believe that you are the Messiah, the Son of God, the one coming into the world" (John 11:25-27).

Martha now goes back to the home not expecting anything to happen, except some day in the future, and when Martha told Mary that Jesus had arrived she immediately got up and went to find him. The others in the home followed her thinking she was going to the tomb to weep. As she approached Jesus who was still in the same place as if waiting for her, she came and knelt before him saying the same words as Martha, "Lord, if you had been here my brother would not have died." As she spoke these words the scriptures tell us she was weeping uncontrollably.

Now when Jesus saw her weeping and the crowd of people who had come with her weeping we are told that he was "greatly disturbed in spirit and deeply moved." These words in the original Greek are difficult to translate. They indicate that Jesus was deeply moved almost to the point of anger. Why anger? Jesus was surrounded by sorrow and this would be no gentle shedding of tears. There must have been an almost hysterical wailing and shrieking, for from the people's point of view, the more demonstrative the emotions, the more they would honor the one who had died. The original language tells us that Jesus groaned outwardly like the snorting of a horse and that he was so distressed in spirit that his body trembled.

Having officiated at hundreds of funerals through the years I have discovered that the depth of sorrow expressed is related to the closeness of the family members and to the age of the person who died. When a person in their nineties sleeps away into death after a long and faithful life, the funeral becomes one of sorrow like the sorrow of a farewell, but it is also a time of rejoicing and celebration of life.

In our parish in Nevada, Iowa, following a football game, a high school student rushed home to change clothes for a party at someone's home. He never arrived at the party because in his rush to get there he went through a stop sign and was killed in a sudden crash. At the emergency ward in the hospital where the body was taken, I met with the family. There was such deep grief and shock that words and thoughts were difficult to express. I literally groaned within. How inadequate one can feel and one could only pray that just being there was a presence of beginning comfort and strength. At the funeral the grief was so intense it was like you could cut the air with a knife. Following the graveside committal, however, one could see the beginning of healing comfort as the young man's classmates came up to the parents one by one giving them a hug and a special flower. Once again I wept and groaned within.

Jesus and Mary and Martha and their friends formed a procession to the cemetery and the cave in which Lazarus was buried. When Jesus asked for the stone to be rolled away Martha was surprised and said, "Lord, already there is a stench because he has been dead for four days" (John 11:39). The Jews believed that after a person died the spirit would hover around the body and when decay began to set in after three days the spirit would leave. No question about it, Lazarus was dead! Now Jesus cries out, "Lazarus, come out!" We read that "the dead man came out, his hands and feet bound with strips of cloth, and his face wrapped in a cloth" (John 11:44). Binding and strapping were part of the usual Jewish customs of the day. Instead of walking out of the tomb Lazarus must have staggered and stumbled out into the light of day. The story ends suddenly with Jesus commanding: "Unbind him and let him go."

Lazarus became for the crowds around Jerusalem a walking, breathing, talking miracle of new life after death. So we read in the scriptures, "When the great crowd of the Jews learned that Lazarus was there [Bethany], they came not only because of Jesus but also to see Lazarus, whom he had raised from the dead. So the chief priests planned to put Lazarus to death as well [as Jesus], since it was on account of him that many of the Jews were deserting and were believing in Jesus" (John 12:9-11).

Although Lazarus was raised from the dead his body was not the new body that we will have in the resurrection. His body was still flesh and blood. Lazarus died again! If the death of Lazarus were the end of the story we would never know about this miracle or any of the other signs of Jesus, and you, my friend, would not be reading this book and we would not be a part of any Christian church except for one tremendous fact. Jesus, our Lord, suffered and died and was buried in a cave in Joseph's garden with a great stone sealing its entrance. On the third day after his death with a great earthquake the stone was rolled away. Jesus lived again and his new body was not flesh and blood. No, it was a body like the one we will have in the resurrection, a body that will live forever and ever. The greatest miracle and sign of all is that Jesus died, rose again, and lives! The Apostle Paul, who experienced this living Jesus on the road to Damascus, was dramatically changed into a witness more alive than ever and was enabled to write to the Christians at Rome, and to us, the words: "If you confess with your lips that Jesus is Lord and believe in your heart that God raised him from the dead you will be saved" (Romans 10:9).

It was Jesus who said those liberating words, "Unbind him, and let him go." One of the most amazing things about the abundant life here and now is that we can live each day in faith. There are times in which we are overwhelmed with grief, overwhelmed with problems and cares, and overwhelmed with uncertainty and the fear of death. Then Jesus comes and lifts our faith and gives us a vision of a life yet to be. It is this Jesus who unbinds us and sets us free.

One of my favorite professional golfers through the years has been Lee Trevino. As I get older and the aches, pains, and stiffness of joints limit my own golf game, I think of the words he would often say: "The older I get, the better I used to be." Some years ago he was struck by lightning while playing in a tournament. In describing the experience he said, "When I got killed by lightning I realized the passage from life is a tremendous pleasure." Lee Trevino was sitting under a tree when lightning hit. "It bolted my arms and legs out stiff, jerked me off the ground," he recalls, "and killed me. I knew I was dead. There was no pain. Everything turned a warm, gentle orange color. I saw my mama who had been dead for years. I saw other people from my life. It was a newsreel like you read about — my life passing before my eyes. But it was so pleasant, so wonderful, I felt great. I thought, boy this dying is really fun. It's when I woke up in the hospital badly burned and in pain that I knew that I had come back to life again for some reason." Eternal life begins in the here and now when Jesus is our Lord and Savior. Death cannot separate us from his love. Lee Trevino said after his experience, "There's no reason to fear death."[3]

Recently my father-in-law, Ray Johnson, died at the age of 94 in a nursing home in Lamberton, Minnesota. He just slipped away into death as he slept late one afternoon. When I heard about the death of Ray I thought of the words of an unknown poet whom I have quoted through the years, "Lord, grant that I might slip away, as slips the night into the day, so softly, that those watching can only say, here ends the night, and there begins the day."

His death came in the midst of the coldest part of a Minnesota winter. Since the family was scattered and many couldn't make a funeral at that time, a short committal service was held at the cemetery, and plans were made for a memorial service to be held in the summer at Hope Lutheran Church in Walker, Minnesota. This church was close to Ten Mile Lake where Ray and his family had spent summers for years. Ray was a very important man to me. Having grown up without a father he became like my own father. He accepted me into the family and treated me as one of his own. When I was asked to officiate at this service I accepted with fear and trepidation. How I prayed that I would be able to control the great depth of my own emotions.

Since Winston Churchill was one of the heroes in Ray's life I chose to tell a story about him and his own funeral. Certainly Churchill as the great leader of Great Britain, as well as the Western world during World War II days, inspired and lifted up the courage of millions with his resonant and eloquent voice, as well as his deep and abiding faith.

Before Churchill died he made out detailed plans for his funeral that were found in his files and were then carefully followed. The funeral was held at the great St. Paul's Cathedral in London. The Anglican Liturgy which Churchill loved was used. Hymns were sung and scriptures read that he had chosen. At the end of the funeral a remarkable thing happened under his directions. A bugler had been stationed at one end of the great dome of the Cathedral. At the end of the funeral he stood and played "Taps," the universal evening song symbolizing death and the end of the day. But Churchill was too much of a theologian and believer to have his funeral end on such a note, and when "Taps" had sounded there was silence and the sounds of mourning. Then another bugler at the other end of the dome played "Reveille," the universal song of the morning announcing the beginning of a new day. At Ray's funeral, Al Griggs, a great musician and trumpet player and longtime friend of the family, was there. It seemed significant to me that at the end of Ray's memorial service he played "Taps" and then "Reveille," for Ray's faith in our Lord was deep and all of us knew that he really had slipped away into death and then into the most abundant life of all.[4]

It is my hope and prayer that all who read this including my own children and my children's children would know Jesus as Lord, and as the greatest instrument of life the world has ever known. You, too, can experience those qualities of life that really make us alive. You, too, can experience *joy, trust, hope, nourishment, peace, sight and insight, and new life like a grain of wheat.* You and I can hear this Jesus say to us daily, "I came that you may have life, and have it abundantly."

Reflection And Discussion

Thought Questions

1. Why would Jesus delay going to Bethany when he heard about Lazarus?

2. What was the situation when Jesus arrived in Bethany?

3. What were the emotions of Jesus when he came to the cemetery?

4. How does the resurrection of Lazarus give us new life?

5. How do you feel if someone you love disappoints you and lets you down?

Agree Or Disagree

- Weeping at a funeral is a sign of weakness.

- The resurrection of Lazarus was the same as the resurrection of Jesus.

- More people would believe today if someone was resurrected from the dead.

Endnotes

1. Study on time at University of Wisconsin from old notes, source unknown.
2. William Barclay, *The New Daily Bible Study, The Gospel of John*, Vol. 2 (Louisville: Westminster John Knox Press, 1975), pp. 80-103.
3. Willie Nelson with Bud Shrake, *Willie, An Autobiography* (New York: Simon & Schuster, 1988), pp. 218-219.
4. Winston Churchill story contributed, source unknown.

Other Resources

V. Eugene Johnson, *The Seven Signs in the Gospel of John* (Rock Island, Illinois: Augustana Book Concern, 1955), pp. 62-71.

Robert Kysar, *Augsburg Commentary on the New Testament* (Minneapolis: Augsburg Publishing House, 1986), pp. 172-184.

Roger L. Fredrikson, *The Communicator's Commentary — John* (Waco: Word Books, 1985), pp. 191-200.

Index Of Illustrations

Bread/Nourishment
attitude of Dylan Davis	62
beauty and Mojave Desert	57
Bishop Paul Werger	63
bread and music	57
bread in the Middle East	55
bread in the time of Jesus	55
death of a youth	56
Dr. Kenneth G. Haugk	61
Dr. Larry Dossey	58
Gentle Ted, distributing	54
Martin Luther and bread	62
mixing up numbers	54
nourishment of crust	56
out-of-control wants	63
Pastor Daniel Martin	59
quilt women	60
returning Bobbie	61
spoonerisms	52
television	63

Hope
dead mule on front yard	44
Dr. George Forell	42
Dr. Philip C. McGraw	41
Pablo Casals	46
pulling up stakes	45
rats swimming	43
senior ailments	39

Joy
Albert Schweitzer	26
avoiding a ticket	18
belly laughing	18
choosing joy	17
joy and rain	13

Norman Cousins	19
wedding embarrassment	15

Marriage
marriage plaque	32
tax assessor and property	66
three women, bad memory	65
tired man and package	64
wedding problems	15, 32

New Life
funerals	102
Lee Trevino	106
light in the window	100
old shoe ticket	97
stained glass windows and wheat	99
study on time and waiting	42, 101
sudden death of student	104
village of Bethany	100
waiting and shingles	101
weeping	104
Winston Churchill funeral	107

Peace
Amy and Jamie	74
antidote for worry	75
commercial pilot and landing	73
first aid for stress	75
painting of peace	71
painting of Peter	72
Pastor Charles Allen	76
skater Dan Janson	77
storms on the prairie	69
ten most stressful events	74

Sight and Insight

Annabelle Costanzo	89
blind Stanley	90
blind Susan	83
blindsight	85
bumper stickers	87
Cambodian refugees	85
Helen Keller	89
nearsighted James	86

Trust

boy and teakettle	26
congregational trust	33
Golden Wedding words	32
Robert Kysar	29
singing in youth choir	27
son Jon and refrigerator	28
trust and Pastor Moe	30
trusting caretaker	31
trusting painters	29

Endorsements

Finding and using apt illustrations to enhance a sermon or Bible study is a fine art. In this book, Forrest Chaffee proves himself a master at this endeavor. I highly recommend this book to anyone wanting to plumb the depths of some of the most significant miracles of Jesus.
    Herbert Chilstrom
    Former Presiding Bishop
    Evangelical Lutheran Church in America

This book is a beautiful witness to the possibilities of a deeper and richer spiritual life. Chaffee opens up for us the spiritual wisdom of John's Gospel in understandable simplicity.
    Jerry L. Schmalenberger
    Former President
    Pacific Lutheran Theological Seminary

Forrest Chaffee opens up the signs of John's Gospel to us as he also opens up his own life and experiences for us to behold. Pastors and laypersons alike will enjoy his rich storytelling abilities. This engaging work, deeply rooted in a faithful pastor's heart, is a resource that will surely help others grow in their faith — and become more alive than ever!
    Daniel Solomon
    Senior Pastor, Augustana Lutheran Church
    Boone, Iowa

In its sensitivity and simplicity, Forrest Chaffee's pastoral style penetrates to the heart of the Fourth Gospel's theology, which is the sacramental nature of all life. Both the Evangelist and Pastor Chaffee encourage readers to find God in the immediacy of daily existence.
    Edward W. Amend
    Emeritus Professor of Religion and Humanities
    University of Northern Iowa

www.ingramcontent.com/pod-product-compliance
Lightning Source LLC
Chambersburg PA
CBHW071714040426
42446CB00011B/2066